Employers' Use of Flexible Labour

Policy Studies Institute (PSI) is one of Europe's leading independent research organisations undertaking studies of economic, industrial and social policy and the workings of political institutions.

PSI is a registered charity, run on a non-profit basis, and is not associated with any political party, pressure group or commercial interest.

PSI attaches great importance to covering a wide range of subject areas with its multidisciplinary approach. The Institute's researchers are organised in groups which currently cover the following programmes:

Crime, Justice and Youth Studies – Employment – Ethnic Equality and Diversity – Family Finances – Information and Citizenship – Information and Cultural Studies – Social Care and Health Studies – Work, Benefits and Social Participation

This publication arises from the Employment Group and is one of over 30 publications made available by the Institute each year.

Information about the work of PSI and a catalogue of publications can be obtained from:
Publications Department, Policy Studies Institute, 100 Park Village East, London NW1 3SR

Employers' Use of Flexible Labour

Bernard Casey, Hilary Metcalf and Neil Millward

POLICY STUDIES INSTITUTE

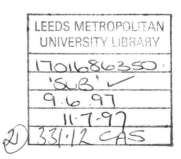

The publishing imprint of the independent
POLICY STUDIES INSTITUTE
100 Park Village East, London NW1 3SR
Tel. 0171 468 0468   Fax. 0171 388 0914

ISBN 0 85374 712 1   X 20 5267083
PSI Report 837

PSI publications are available from:
BEBC Distribution Ltd, P O Box 1496, Poole, Dorset BH12 3YD

Books will normally be dispatched within 24 hours. Cheques should be made payable to BEBC Distribution Ltd.

Credit cards and telephone/fax orders may be placed on the following freephone numbers:
FREEPHONE   0800 262260
FREEFAX   0800 262266

Booktrade representation (UK and Eire):
Broadcast Books, 24 De Montfort Road, London SW16 1LZ
Tel. 0181 677 5129

PSI subscriptions are available from PSI's subscription agent:
Carfax Publishing Company Ltd,
P O Box 25, Abingdon, Oxford OX14 3UE

Laserset by Policy Studies Institute
Printed in Great Britain by Redwood Books, Trowbridge, Wiltshire

Contents

Tables

Acknowledgements

We would like to thank all those who contributed to this book. Thanks are due to the Department for Education and Employment who commissioned the research, of which this book is the outcome. We would also like to thank the employers who participated in the study and who gave their time so generously to discuss their employment practices. Last, but not least, we would like to thank Lauren Bergida, Cornell University, who gave invaluable assistance in setting up the case studies.

Summary

This study examines an important aspect of labour market 'flexibility'. It looks at how employers make short-term quantitative adjustments to their labour supply in response to changes in demand and other factors.

Approach

The study focuses on working arrangements that involve non-standard patterns of working time – arrangements other than full-time work with fixed weekly hours at regular times. With varying degrees of emphasis it looks at:

- part-time working;
- temporary and casual working;
- work involving varying weekly hours; and
- shift working.

Each of these can provide a degree of 'numerical flexibility'.

The study addresses four questions, namely:

- whether the incidence of non-standard arrangements has increased since 1984;
- whether the variety of non-standard arrangements has increased;
- what reasons and circumstances lead employers to the use of each of the various forms of non-standard working; and
- what, if any, changes in patterns of use could be expected in the future.

Two main methods were employed in the research:

- analysis of two large-scale survey series: the Labour Force Surveys of spring 1994, the three preceding quarters and spring 1984; and the Workplace Industrial Relations Surveys of 1984 and 1990.
- the conduct of twenty four case studies in six industries – clothing, oil refining, metal goods, hotels and catering, business services and health – industries which either made extensive use of non-standard arrangements or had experienced a substantial growth in the use of them.

Principal findings

The most widely used form of short-term 'numerical flexibility' is variation of employees' hours of work from week to week. This occurs principally by salaried employees working varying amounts of 'unpaid overtime' and waged employees doing varying amounts of paid overtime; but it also includes much rarer arrangements such as 'zero-hours contracts'.

More than half of all employees work variable numbers of hours from week to week.

This form of 'flexibility' is not new, but its incidence among employees has nearly doubled over the past decade. Temporary working also increased over the decade, but less dramatically. So did part-time working, although this is less clearly 'flexible' from the employer's point of view.

The growth in these three forms of 'flexible' working over the past decade has arisen not from the growing importance of industries and occupations where they already prevailed, but a greater intensity of use across the board. This increase in intensity has been greater in larger and medium sized establishments than in small ones – contrary to the widely-held view that the spread of small establishments was mainly responsible for the growth in 'flexibility'.

In most workplaces the majority of the workforce is full-time on fixed hours. It is rare for employers to use several of the main forms of flexible non-standard employment at the same workplace. For example, only four per cent of workplaces use both short-term contract workers and freelancers.

Workplaces which used several types of non-standard employment together tended to be those where labour costs dominated production costs. They also tended to be newer workplaces.

Part of the increase in the use of both freelancers and short-term contract workers may reflect the decline in trade unions' ability to resist their use by employers.

Aggregate national statistics on the use of different types of 'flexible' labour, which are regrettably incomplete, reflect widely different patterns of use by individual employers in distinct workplaces. Among the factors affecting employers' choices on what types of employment arrangement to offer employees are: the variability of demand for the final product (through the day, week, month and year); the way in which the production has been organised in the past (including the gender division of labour); the importance of labour costs in total cost; the salience of the quality and timeliness of outputs; the constraints and opportunities presented by the external labour market; and the attitudes and morale of employees and their representatives. Each of these factors can influence the use the made of 'flexible' labour, but rarely in a deterministic fashion.

Some employers attempt to modify the variability of their demand in order to reduce the need for flexible working time arrangements to minimise costs. Others achieve similar ends by modifying the mix of skills held by different groups of employees – an alternative form of 'flexibility'.

As circumstances change, so working-time practices are likely to change. However, employers rarely standardize on a single set of working-time practices for a given set of circumstances; moreover, their response to the same set of circumstances can vary over time. Some of the more innovative working arrangements appear to have spread from 'leading edge' firms; others have not been adopted more widely because managers know little of them or how they could be applied.

Employers will continue to innovate in this field. But it is difficult to forecast their changing use of different types of non-standard working time arrangement – and, indeed, other forms of labour market 'flexibility' – not only because of the wide variety of factors that influence their use but also because we have very partial information about them.

Recommendations

The best national survey datasets currently available are inadequate for understanding, let alone forecasting, developments in the labour market with respect to working time and associated matters. While case studies can provide useful indications and illustrations, the most pressing need is for a new, large-scale survey of employers' practices, building on the lessons learnt from this study and other research.

Such a survey would enable policy makers, and others with an interest in the operations of the labour market, to understand better the nature of jobs available (including their degree of permanence), the skills and training required to do them, the segregation of men and women within employment, the scope for 'family friendly' employment, and the preparedness of unemployed people to take up paid work.

Selected waves of the Labour Force Survey should include newly developed questions on working-time arrangements and non-standard contractual arrangements, in particular on the variability of working hours from day to day and week to week.

Chapter 1

literature
review

Introduction

Labour market analysts, employment specialists and policy makers have adopted the notion of 'labour market flexibility' almost universally in recent years. 'Flexibility' is hardly a neutral word and when it is coupled so frequently with phrases like 'improved economic growth' or 'national economic competitiveness' it carries powerful positive connotations in most quarters. Few of the synonyms for flexibility have negative associations: adaptability, responsiveness, adjustability, resilience and so on all seem like characteristics of the national labour market that everyone should want there to be more of. Naturally, adaptations in labour market behaviour and employment practices are needed to cope with external changes that cannot effectively be resisted. Few would argue, for instance, that global economic forces and shifts in the pattern of world trade can effectively be resisted by British employers and employees alone. At this level, flexibility is almost incontestably 'a good thing'.

At more detailed levels of analysis, flexibility in relation to labour market behaviour approaches contested ground. In terms of 'functional flexibility', some employers may want a core of workers with a broad range of skills, even to be 'multi-skilled', whilst others may prefer people with a well-defined set of skills – as encapsulated by the notion of occupation or trade. Workers too have varying preferences about the range of tasks they may be called upon to do; some like to 'stick to the knitting', whilst others relish the challenge of unfamiliar tasks. Some may prefer working in teams, whilst others do not. In terms of 'numerical flexibility', employers may want to cut employment to a minimum and to have a flexible labour market in which they can quickly respond to changes in the demand for their products or services by hiring or shedding labour. Employees, on the other hand, may value employment stability. Not all employees and all employers will want the same things. Some employers may have relatively stable environments and prefer a stable, but adaptable, workforce. Some employees may prefer the variety offered by temporary, employment-agency work or the flexibility of working hours offered by 'flexitime' arrangements.

It is around these notions of 'numerical flexibility' that we focus in this study: the level of the individual employer and employee and the arrangements made between them that impact on the quantities of labour supplied to the employer. For a recent review of, largely economic, evidence on various interpretations of 'labour market flexibility' at the aggregate level, the reader is referred to Beatson (1995).

Our concern in this study is principally centred on *non-standard working-time practices* that allow or create some form of quantitative flexibility of operation or organisation for the employer. By this we mean the use of employment relationships other than the employment of full-time 'permanent' employees for regular and fixed hours. We have included, with varying degrees of emphasis, temporary workers, those on varying hours of work, casual workers, shift working and most forms of part-time employment. The inclusion of part-time employees among the 'flexible' labour force is conventional, although somewhat contentious. A number of arguments can be put forward to justify their inclusion. First, part-time employees give employers more opportunities to alter labour inputs. This arises for two reasons: their turnover rate is generally higher and the employer thus has more opportunities to replace a part-timer with either a full-timer or a part-timer on different hours, or not to replace the part-timer at all; and part-timers are generally easier to dismiss because of their less extensive employment protection rights.[1] Second, because overtime premia are not generally paid until hours exceed the basic full-time hours, part-timers may have their hours increased at lower cost to the employer. Third, because part-timers often receive fewer non-wage benefits than full-timers they may be easier and cheaper for the employer to recruit. Of course, these generalisations do not apply to all part-time work, but they are sufficiently valid in the generality of cases for the convention of including part-timers as part of the flexible labour force to be acceptable for current purposes.⌉

Three issues are addressed. The first is the extent to which there is evidence that non-standard employment relationships, defined in this way, have become more varied in recent years. The second is whether they are becoming increasingly prevalent in the British labour market. The third issue is what circumstances (particularly of employers, but also of employees) give rise to the use of the various forms of non-standard employment relationship. The three issues are interrelated and our discussion will frequently make connections between them.

Recent public debate and published research on non-standard working time has had two distinct strands: one has focused on employers' labour use policies and practices in terms of the efficiency of production; the second has been the growing concern with the relationship between paid employment and domestic life, and especially in the opportunity which non-standard working allows for better reconciliation of these two aspects of adult life. We will temporarily adopt this duality in setting the context for our study and describing how we arrived at our chosen research methods.

Employers' policies and practices on the use of labour

Although the management literature has long had an interest in labour management practices that enabled firms to adapt to changing circumstances, the issue undoubtedly gained increased prominence in the mid-1980s with the publication and wide discussion of the model of the 'flexible firm' put forward by Atkinson and his colleagues (Atkinson, 1985). In essence, the flexible firm divided its labour force into a core of permanent workers performing the key tasks and a periphery of non-standard workers which insulated the core group from changes in demand and other uncertainties. The peripheral workers included people working under a wide variety of non-standard employment conditions such as casual and temporary employees, freelancers and other subcontractors.

There was keen debate in the late 1980s whether flexible (non-standard) working had grown and whether this signalled a new managerial approach (Atkinson and Meager, 1986; Pollert, 1988; Hakim, 1987). The evidence cited was largely drawn from case studies of private sector firms or trends in the employment of particular categories of labour drawn from large-scale surveys of individuals. A major initiative to produce large-scale evidence from employers was launched by the Employment Department in the mid-1980s, incorporating both a large-scale survey and associated case studies. The survey was the Employers' Labour Use Strategies (ELUS) survey of 1987, constructed as a selective (and unrepresentative) follow-up of establishments in the 1984 Workplace Industrial Relations Survey (WIRS); the 49 'case studies' involved a further interview with a manager at a focused selection of establishments from the ELUS survey and were carried out in 1988/89.

The ELUS project concluded that few employers were adopting a new flexibility strategy. Rather, it showed that most non-standard employment was used for traditional reasons, such as the occurrence of peaks in demand within various time periods, to perform tasks of uncertain or limited duration, or the temporary unavailability of full-time, permanent employees (Wood and Smith, 1987; McGregor and Sproull, 1991; Hunter and MacInnes, 1991). More recent reviews of the literature have generally concurred (Beatson, 1995).

The reconciliation of employment and non-working life

The second strand of interest in forms of work which involve non-standard working time has been focused on the labour supply decisions of individuals in specific family and domestic situations. To some observers the growth of non-standard working- time arrangements is the outcome of some types of worker seeking better ways of reconciling their family and domestic roles with paid work. The main focus has been on women, particularly mothers, in relation to childcare and part-time employment; but a wide variety of working arrangements have been seen as satisfying the dual demands of domestic and work life, including temporary work, term-time working and job-sharing. More recently there has been increased interest in the issue of caring for elderly relatives and the types of working arrangement that facilitate this. Both strands of literature have been well reviewed by Brannen and her colleagues (Brannen et al, 1994).

Concern about the 'demographic time bomb' provided one of the stimuli for considering new and different employment and working-time arrangements, prodding employers to seek workers hitherto outside the labour force. Fears of skill shortages led to a greater recognition by government and employers of the costs of women employees leaving the workforce because of childcare (and other) responsibilities. Growing support, some of it from employers, for increased equality of opportunity to work and within work has added further impetus to the debate. Regardless of the aim, developments have focused on extending part-time employment (including school-hours employment), job-sharing and term-time employment.

Whilst less common than arrangements relating to maternity and childcare, non-standard working has also been introduced for older people, to ease the move from employment to retirement and, for the employer, to ease the handover of responsibilities. Some employers have introduced reduced working days or reduced working weeks in the period up to retirement (Casey, Metcalf and Lakey, 1993). New types of contracts (including part-time and self-employed) have also been introduced for workers over retirement age.

Recent developments

Developments in the early 1990s suggested that it would be advantageous to mount a further study of non-standard working practices. Since ELUS was conducted, managerial literature has continued to emphasise flexibility, including the efficiency benefits of non-standard working-time practices. Major organisations are known to have introduced non-standard practices in order to better match demand for their products or services with availability of labour (for example, lunchtime hours for bank branch staff, a switch to part-time employment for retail staff). The use of contracted out services has grown, both in the private and public sector. At the same time, the threat of labour shortage and the demographic time-bomb have receded.

Using a broad definition, the 'flexible workforce' has increased steadily in recent years from 30 per cent of the workforce in

1981 to 35 per cent in 1986 and 38 per cent in 1993, according to Labour Force Survey estimates (Watson, 1994). The broad definition of the flexible workforce used in that analysis included part-time employees, temporary workers, the self-employed, people on government training schemes and unpaid family workers – in fact, everyone in employment except full-time, permanent employees. Most of the growth was in self-employment. Among employees, part-time workers increased in numbers while full-time workers hardly increased at all. From the employers' point of view, many of the categories of 'flexible worker' included in this broad definition do not necessarily increase flexibility over labour. Only temporary workers incontestably do so in comparison with permanent workers. Temporary workers increased only slightly in numbers during the 1980s (Casey, 1991), but more rapidly in the early 1990s, reaching a total of 1.5 million in Spring 1995, compared with 1.25 million in 1983.

Thus, both broad and narrow definitions of the flexible workforce have shown an increase in recent years. Further understanding of why this growth has occurred was considered to be desirable. In particular, it was thought to be advantageous to know whether it arose from substantial changes in employers' labour utilisation practices or whether it merely reflected shifts in employment to sectors where the use of 'flexible' labour was most common.

The aims of the project

Against this broader background of the changing labour market, the (then) Employment Department funded a study to shed further light on recent developments in the use of non-standard and flexible working-time practices *by employers*. In particular, it sought to establish whether new practices or employers' rationales for using non-standard labour were in evidence. More specifically, the study sought to explore:

- the extent to which non-standard working practices were used in different types of workplace;
- changes over time in the use of non-standard working practices by different types of workplace;

- employers' reasons for using various non-standard working practices and for changes in their level and use over time;
- the perceived advantages and disadvantages to employers of the different types of working-time practice and employment contract;
- the constraints which employers face on exercising greater flexibility in the use of labour;
- likely future trends in the use of non-standard work arrangements.

Finally, the project aimed to identify themes and issues that might be addressed in future large-scale quantitative research.

Research methods

Given that a great deal of information was already available about the issues of interest and that no major data collection initiative was possible within the resources available, it was decided that the project could most usefully address its aims by using two main methods. One would be secondary analysis of relevant existing large-scale datasets. The other would be new case study work in a range of establishments, selected as having a variety of the practices of interest. These two methods are briefly discussed in turn.

Secondary analysis of existing datasets

The datasets which were selected for further analysis were: the *Workplace Industrial Relations Surveys* (WIRS), which refers to employers; and the *Labour Force Surveys* (LFS) which refers to individuals. Both collect nationally representative data and, as survey series, offer the opportunity for analysis of change over time.

The *Workplace Industrial Relations Surveys* provide information on the use of non-standard working practices at the level of the employing establishment. The surveys have very extensive information on the characteristics of establishments (or workplaces) and some information on the larger organisations of which most workplaces are a part. The two most recent surveys in the series, conducted in 1984 and 1990, were considered to be of most relevance. The 1990 survey, although somewhat out of date, is the most recent large-scale national survey of workplaces

7

that permits an examination of current practices, and comparisons with the previous survey to a very similar design allowed some investigation of changes in the pattern over time. In addition, the WIRS series had the very clear benefit of having a panel sample of workplaces interviewed in both 1984 and 1990, which permitted some exploration of changes within the same establishments over the six-year period.

The WIRS series was not conceived as a survey focusing on non-standard working-time practices, and the data within it are confined to only some of the practices of interest in this study. It has information on the use of part-time employees, people employed on short fixed-term contracts, freelancers and homeworkers/outworkers. For most groups of employee there is some information on the extent of overtime working. WIRS allows the incidence and intensity of these practices to be mapped across different types of workplace. Comparisons of the two cross-sectional samples and the panel dataset permit changes in their use to be charted.

An additional advantage of the surveys is that they contain information on the broader managerial and economic context in which non-standard working practices are used. Using WIRS it is possible to examine the relationship between non-standard working time practices and other non-standard practices such as subcontracting, reduced job-demarcation and multi-skilling. There is also some scope for investigating the potential for introducing such practices, through reporting on managers' views of the potential for reorganising work.

Further discussion of the advantages and disadvantages of the WIRS series as a resource for examining employers' use of flexible employment practices and non-standard labour is given at the beginning of Chapter 3.

The *Labour Force Surveys* are the most extensive and longest standing source of national statistics on non-standard working with respect to individuals. They contain some information on personal characteristics and a good deal on the characteristics of the individual's current job (or main job), including whether it is part-time or full-time, seen as permanent or temporary by the individual, and so on. Whilst it does not permit analysis of the use of non-standard working by any characteristics of the employer or the employee's workplace (other than industry and size), it complements the WIRS information by having data on a wider range of non-standard working forms.

Until recently, the types of non-standard working identified by the LFS were temporary work, part-time employment, irregular hours of work, and shift working. Recent surveys in the series have collected further information with a new question on working-time practices which allow employees different, and possibly more convenient or more flexible, arrangements than conventional full-time working for a standard and fixed number of hours. These include flexitime, annualised hours, term-time working and job-sharing. This detailed question is too recent to permit examination of changes in these practices over time and it is asked too infrequently to do any seasonal analysis. Early analysis of the pattern of use of these practices have been reported in Watson (1994).

The main issues addressed in the LFS analysis were to be the industrial variation in the main types of flexible labour, changes over the previous ten years, seasonal variations and the various combinations of flexible working characteristics.

Case studies

The second element of the research design involved new empirical work using qualitative methods. Twenty-four case studies were conducted to explore the issues underlying the different labour-use patterns identified in each employing organisation or establishment. The issues to be addressed included:

- the reasons for using various non-standard working practices and for changes in their level of use over time;
- the perceived advantages and disadvantages of the different types of working practices (including full-time, permanent contracts) and combinations of their use within the same employing unit;
- the constraints which employers face in exercising greater flexibility in the use of labour;
- likely future trends in the use of non-standard work arrangements.

Within the case studies, the use of non-standard working practices was examined in the context of other flexible practices, the substitutability between practices and the scope for change in the organisation (including management and employee constraints).

The cases studies involved semi-structured interviews with employers at the director or senior manager level, using a topic guide drawn up in consultation with researchers at the (then) Employment Department and informed by the quantitative research. The selection of the case study organisations was based upon a number of considerations, the main ones being to choose organisations in a variety of industries which either had extensive use of non-standard working or had shown growth in it. The reasons for the selections are set out more fully in Chapter 4, which introduces the qualitative part of the study.

The structure of the book

Chapters 2 and 3 respectively report the results of the analysis of the Labour Force Surveys and the Workplace Industrial Relations Surveys. Chapter 4 describes how the case studies were selected and sketches the characteristics of those where interviews took place. The actual practices in use, and management's rationales for them, are the focus of Chapter 5, while Chapter 6 takes a broader look at the whole range of practices covered in the cases studies and managers' views of the reasons for using and not using them. Chapter 7 examines the case study evidence on the possible future use of the different practices, and managers' plans for change in the light of anticipated changes in the circumstances of their employing organisation. In Chapter 8 we draw our main conclusions from the analysis in Chapters 2 to 7, with suggestions about the future focus of research on employers' use of 'flexible' employment arrangements.

Note

1   Under the terms of the Employment Protection (Consolidation) Act of 1978, employees working under 16 but no fewer than 8 hours per week were required to have completed five years' service before they qualified for protection against unfair dismissal, rather than the two years which applied to employees working 16 or more hours, and those working under 8 hours did not qualify at all. However, the Employment Protection (Part-time Employees) Regulations of 1995 has placed all part-timers on the same footing as full-timers.

Chapter 2

Evidence from the
Labour Force Surveys

The Labour Force Survey (LFS) is the largest, longest running and most widely used source of statistical information about the employment and labour market behaviour of individuals in the UK economy. It is a quarterly sample survey covering some 60,000 households and was conducted every two years until 1983 and annually thereafter. It thus lends itself to the analysis not only of current employment practices but also of changes in practice over time. Although it provides information on individuals, rather than employers, it can show the extent to which particular forms of labour are used. It is particularly useful for showing the occupations and industrial sectors in which non-standard labour is used most intensively. A distinct advantage is its comprehensive coverage of people working in all sizes and types of establishment and organisation, and the inclusion of individuals working in small establishments also makes it an important complement to the Workplace Industrial Relations Surveys analysed in Chapter 3, which exclude small establishments.

Recent studies of flexible labour forms using the LFS have focused on part-time employment (Naylor, 1994) and analysed the questions introduced in the Spring 1993 survey on additional forms of flexibility: flexitime, annual hours, term-time working, job-sharing and compressed working weeks (Watson, 1994). In this chapter we update some of that analysis using more recent LFS results, and add some additional themes, including seasonality in the use of flexible labour and its incidence in small establishments.

Given our focus in this study upon the ways in which employers use non-standard or flexible labour and working-time arrangements, the analysis concentrates upon employees in employment (the dependent labour force) and thus ignores, with two exceptions, the self-employed. Among employees, the following flexible employment forms can be identified:

- *part-time employees* – people who define themselves as having less than full-time jobs, regardless of the actual hours they normally work;
- *temporary employees* – people who define their jobs as being available only for a limited (if not always specified) period of time;
- *agency workers* – a sub-category of temporary workers who are leased out by a temporary work bureau and who remain the employee of that bureau rather than of the company where they are placed;
- *employees whose hours vary from week to week* – either as a result of their working variable amounts of overtime (paid or unpaid) or because their hours vary for some other reason;
- *employees on annual hours contracts* – those whose working time is contracted in terms of an annual rather than a weekly limit.

These categories are not mutually exclusive: employers may, for example, employ a person on a temporary, part-time basis. Indeed, many of the arrangements may be combined and part-time hours can certainly be combined with any of the other arrangements. The main combinations are discussed in a later section of this chapter.

Details of a number of other non-traditional working-time arrangements are now included in the LFS. These are flexitime, term-time working, job-sharing, nine-day fortnights and four-and-a-half day weeks. At the time of the study, only the first survey covering these practices was available. As this has already been analysed by Watson (1994), it does not feature in this study.

In addition to employees, two groups of self-employed workers were of interest, since they provide an alternative or additional source of labour for employers:

- *labour-only subcontractors* – unfortunately these cannot be identified directly within the LFS, but *new* labour-only subcontractors can be identified as those who, from one year to the next, stayed in the same occupation and worked in the same firm and who, over that period, moved from being an employee to being self-employed;
- *homeworkers* – who were identified as those working at, or from, home, who were working for an outside employer (rather than a family firm or business) and who were not working on their own account.[1]

LFS data on most of these seven flexible forms of employment are available over the period 1984 to 1994. The exceptions are annual hours contracts and homeworking which have been asked about since only 1993. These limitations mean that the whole range of comparisons through time, seasonally and for the most recent period cannot be made.

A further restriction on the depth of possible analysis arises from changes in the system of classifying the industrial activity of the individual's employer. The move from the 1980 to the 1992 Standard Industrial Classification for the 1993 LFS, restricts the analysis by sector that can be carried out over time. Nevertheless a consistent series for 28 different industrial groups is feasible and has been the basis of our analysis by industry.[2]

Lastly, it has to be pointed out that respondents to the LFS were generally assumed to be able to recognise the terms used in the survey questions that asked about the different arrangements. Thus, in relation to the more unusual working-time arrangements first asked about in 1993, LFS interviewers were told that 'if a respondent asks what is meant by the terms [such as annualised hours] it is unlikely that they will have any of these working hours arrangements' and the interviewer was instructed to code the respondent as having none of them (Watson, 1994). The possibility of substantial measurement errors in the results cannot therefore be ruled out.

Overall use of flexible workers

The overall extent of the different categories of flexible worker in Spring 1994 is shown by industrial sector in Table 2.1.[3] The

13

Table 2.1   Incidence of flexible forms of labour by industry, Spring 1994
(labour forms as percentage of total employment)

Row percentages

Industry	Part-time employees	Temporary employees	Flexible forms (not mutually exclusive)					
			Variable hours workers	Annual hours	Agency temps	'New' labour only sub-contractors	Home workers
Agriculture	20.7	7.7	68.8	3.0	*	1.0	0.5
Oil & gas extraction	3.1	9.0	70.3	4.8	*	*	1.6
Other mining	3.3	8.2	56.3	7.6	*	*	*
Food, drink & tobacco	12.7	3.4	57.9	5.7	*	*	*
Textiles	11.1	2.3	41.9	6.5	*	*	2.4
Leather	16.1	1.6	38.3	5.0	*	*	2.7
Wood products	7.8	3.7	51.3	3.7	*	*	*
Paper, printing & publishing	12.3	4.7	60.0	5.2	*	*	1.4
Oil refining & fuels	3.8	6.5	63.3	12.4	0.9	*	0.7
Chemicals	5.0	6.1	59.0	6.7	*	*	*
Rubber & plastic	8.5	3.0	59.0	7.9	0.5	*	0.5
Other mineral products	4.5	2.5	57.9	8.5	0.5	*	*
Metal products & metals	5.5	2.3	58.8	4.7	*	*	*
Machinery & equipment	5.6	3.6	60.5	6.5	*	*	*
Electrical equipment	6.7	4.7	58.9	4.7	0.6	*	1.2
Transport equipment	2.6	3.7	55.7	6.3	*	*	*

continued

Table 2.1   continued

Row percentages

| | Part-time employees | Temporary employees | Flexible forms (not mutually exclusive) | | | | |
			Variable hours workers	Annual hours	Agency temps	'New' labour only sub-contractors	Home workers
Industry							
Other manufacturing	7.4	2.7	54.8	5.8	0.5	*	1.8
Electricity, gas & water	5.9	5.6	65.8	5.1	*	*	*
Construction	8.0	6.2	58.2	4.6	*	1.5	*
Distribution	39.9	4.0	48.7	4.0	*	*	*
Hotels & restaurants	54.1	10.6	57.4	3.3	*	*	0.6
Transport & communication	9.9	4.6	66.8	5.7	*	*	*
Financial services	14.5	3.4	56.7	3.9	*	*	*
Business services	22.5	7.1	57.8	4.0	0.5	0.5	1.0
Public administration	14.1	5.8	62.2	4.8	*	*	*
Education	36.9	15.8	56.0	19.3	*	*	*
Health & social work	46.3	7.3	51.9	6.8	*	*	0.6
Other services	39.3	11.5	56.1	4.8	*	*	1.5
All industries[a]	**25.4**	**6.5**	**56.3**	**6.2**	**0.2**	**0.3**	**0.6**

* = less than 0.5 per cent
[a] excludes unclassifiable cases

Source: Spring 1994 LFS

'all industries' figures show that the dominant form is clearly *employees whose hours of work vary from week to week,* either because they work varying amounts of overtime or because their basic hours of work are flexible. Such employees constituted as much as 56 per cent of the British workforce in 1994. These include 16 per cent of employees who reported working fewer hours than normal in the reference week because of fewer than usual overtime hours. Unfortunately, the LFS did not ask a similar question of those who worked more hours than usual in the reference week. It is therefore not possible to assess the extent to which the total of those whose hours vary is made up of those working variable amounts of overtime, and those whose hours varied from one week to another for other reasons. However, it seems likely that variable overtime is a substantial, if not the major, part of the total. Thus, a major traditional form of numerical flexibility available to employers – the use of overtime – appears still to provide the most extensive means of varying labour inputs.[4] Whether or not there has been a growth in the number of employees whose basic hours, as opposed to overtime hours, vary from week to week is not possible to say, since there is no long-established series charting their number. However, by examining responses to the recent additional question on patterns of working hours, it is evident that employees on standard working-time arrangements formed the majority of the category; 70 per cent of them had neither flexitime, annualised hours, term-time working, job-sharing, nine-day fortnights nor four-and-a-half day week arrangements.

The second most common type of flexible employment arrangement was *part-time working,* applying to 25 per cent of employees in 1994. Employees whose hours of work varied, and part-time employees, dominate the picture numerically; no other form of flexible employment applied to as much as a tenth of the workforce.

Temporary employees, the most obviously flexible category mentioned so far, were the third most common and represented 7 per cent of employees. They were almost matched in numerical terms by employees on annual hours contracts, who formed 6 per cent of the workforce. None of the other three arrangements included in the analysis covered as much as one per cent of employees.

Differences between industries

In terms of variation across industries, the major form of flexible labour – *employees whose hours of work vary* – exhibited less variation than many of the less widespread forms. The range was from 38 per cent to 70 per cent. 'Textiles' and 'leather' stand out as having relatively low proportions, 42 and 38 per cent respectively; 'agriculture etc', 'oil and gas', and 'transport and communication' have the highest proportions each, close to 70 per cent. Two characteristics would appear to be associated with these differences: the gender mix of the workforce and the extent of shift working. Women form a larger proportion of the workforce in 'textiles' and 'leather' than in the economy as a whole and women are far less likely to work overtime hours; fewer people working varying hours is thus to be expected in these two industries. On the other hand 'agriculture etc', 'oil and gas', and 'transport and communication' employ larger proportions of men, among whom overtime and shift working are more common. In agriculture, variations in hours worked from week to week arise from the unpredictability of the weather and the changing tasks through the seasons. In oil and gas and transport and communication, it is common to have continuous and rotating shift working whereby actual working time would vary from week to week. In oil and gas and in transport and communication, it is common to have continuous and rotating shift working whereby actual working time would vary from week to week. In the transport industry, overtime working is widespread, partly in response to very short-term changes in the demand for services. Apart from these industries with notably low and notably high incidence of employees whose hours of work vary from week to week, the most striking features of this form of flexible working are its high incidence, averaging somewhat over 50 per cent, and its relatively uniform use across most sectors of the economy.

Part-time employment varied much more across industries. Its incidence ranged from as little as 3 per cent of employees in the 'oil and gas', 'other mining' and 'transport equipment manufacture' industries to as much as 54 per cent in 'hotels and restaurants' and close to 50 per cent in 'health and social work'. The industries with very little part-time working are notable for their use of capital intensive production and continuous shift-based working, normally employing men. Generally speaking, part-time employment was much more prevalent in the service sector than in manufacturing, construction and extraction, but not all service sector industries were high users. The highest using industries were ones where activity occurs often outside the 'normal' working day or working week, thus requiring extra part-time staff to cover the additional weekday hours or weekend working. Such jobs are typically taken by women.

Temporary employment also shows widely varying use across industries. It is much more prominent in service industries than in manufacturing, construction or extraction, with the greatest use of temporary workers being found in 'education', 16 per cent, followed by 'other services' and 'hotels and restaurants', 12 and 11 per cent respectively. Each of these industries is characterised by work tasks of limited duration. In the education sector, short courses and research projects are a widespread phenomenon involving the employment of staff on temporary contracts; amongst specific industries included in 'other services' are recreational, cultural and sporting activities, which frequently include one-off events, sometimes involving large numbers of temporary workers; in the case of hotels and catering, one-off events have also traditionally been staffed to a large degree by temporarily engaged workers. Besides these three industrial sectors, 'oil and gas' and 'other mining' also had substantial proportions of temporary workers, again having evident characteristics in terms of the uncertainty of demand and the limited nature of specific tasks that favour temporary employment.

The overall proportion of the labour force made up by *agency workers* was very low: 0.2 per cent. Their use was only substantial in the 'oil refining and fuel' sector, where it approached 1 per cent. For the remainder of the economy, agency workers are spread thinly over the ground.

The proportion of employees reporting that their employment was based upon an annual hours contract was 6 per cent overall, but varied very considerably across the different industries. The highest proportion was in the education sector where 19 per cent of employees said they had such an arrangement. Many teachers and lecturers are contracted to teach specified numbers of hours per year, but it is arguable whether this constitutes an annual hours contract as normally understood in recent usage.[5] Besides education, the two industries with the highest incidence were 'oil refining and fuels' and 'other mineral products', with 12 and 9 per cent respectively. Both industries have a heavy reliance on continuous shift working and common forms of continuous shift plan involve specifying hours on an annual basis.

Lastly, the proportion of workers identifiable as possible 'new' labour-only subcontractors was also very small: 0.3 per cent. Only in the agricultural and construction sectors was the proportion as high as 1 or 2 per cent. The limitation of the LFS in permitting the identification of only *new* members of the category is a severe one. It seems likely, however, that the industries with relatively high proportions of new labour-only subcontractors would also be ones with high numbers of both new and established labour-only subcontractors.

Combinations of forms of flexible labour

As noted earlier, the actual working-time and contractual arrangements that apply to individual employees are more specific that can be captured by a single characteristic such as full-time or part-time, temporary or permanent. Identifying these more specific forms entails combining information from a number of different questions in the LFS. Doing this for all the characteristics discussed so far – full-time or part-time, temporary or permanent, variable or fixed hours, and what forms of variable hours – would be unmanageable. In addition, many of the combinations would be so rare as hardly to merit discussion. Our analysis, therefore, concentrates on the main combinations. Specifically, we focus on the three dichotomies of full-time or part-time, temporary or permanent, variable or fixed hours to identify seven specific forms of flexible labour, plus what is normally regarded as the 'conventional' form of employment. We thus have employees on full-time, permanent, fixed hours, that is, 'conventional' employees plus the following types of 'flexible' labour:

- part-time, permanent, fixed hours
- full-time, temporary, fixed hours
- part-time, temporary, fixed hours

- full-time, permanent, variable hours
- part-time, permanent, variable hours
- full-time, temporary, variable hours
- part-time, temporary, variable hours.

Table 2.2 shows how these various forms of employment were distributed in the economy as a whole, according to the Spring 1994 LFS, and within the industries defined for this analysis.

'Conventional' employees constituted a minority of all employees. That is to say full-time, permanent, fixed hours employees were a minority: they represented only 28 per cent of employees in 1994. They can be regarded as the *numerically* least 'flexible' from the employers' point of view. Industries varied considerably in the proportion of such employees present, with notably high proportions in textiles, leather goods, wood products and transport equipment manufacture – all over 40 per cent. Indeed, nearly all manufacturing industries employed at least a third of their employees under such arrangements. Among non-manufacturing only 'other mining', construction and financial services exceeded one third of their employment on this basis, and several service industries employed considerably fewer than one quarter of their employees as full-time, permanent workers on fixed weekly hours. The industries with the smallest proportions were 'hotels and restaurants' and 'education', each with under 20 per cent.

The most numerous form of flexible labour, and indeed the most numerous of all the categories, was full-time, permanent employees whose hours varied from week to week. These constituted 43 per cent of employees overall. All industries employed substantial numbers of them, while the three industries with the highest proportions were the male-dominated and capital intensive industries of 'oil and gas extraction', 'electricity, gas and water supply' and 'transport and communication'; these all employed at least 60 per cent of their workers as full-time, permanent employees whose hours varied from week to week. The industries with the smallest proportions were 'hotels and restaurants', 'health and social work' and 'distribution'.

The second most numerous form of flexible labour was part-time, permanent, fixed hours employment, accounting for 13 per cent of employees. The use of this form varied much more markedly by industry than the first form mentioned above. Health and social work employed as many as 24 per cent of employees in this way, whereas the capital-intensive extraction industries and 'oil refining and fuels' employed less than 2 per cent of employees under such arrangements. Generally, service industries used higher proportions of part-timers than manufacturing. However, it should be borne in mind that the extent of 'flexibility' offered by part-timers on contracts specifying their working a fixed number of hours per week at fixed times is limited. It might enable peaks of activity to be covered, but it is enhanced if hours can also be shifted around within the week or extended or reduced as required.

There can be few such reservations with the next most numerous form of flexible labour: part-time, permanent employees with variable hours of work. These accounted for 9 per cent of employees overall and were employed in widely varying proportions across industries. Notably high numbers were employed in 'hotels and restaurants', 'health and social work' and 'distribution and repairs'. Most other industries, and all manufacturing industries, employed very few such workers, most of them 5 per cent or less.

Few of the remaining forms of 'flexible' employment accounted for more than 2 per cent of employees in any industry. Temporary, full-time, fixed hours employees were only just over 1 per cent of all employees and did not reach 5 per cent in any of the 28 industries shown separately in Table 2.2. Temporary, part-time, fixed hours employees were also a little over 1 per cent of the total; they approached 5 per cent of employees in education and 3 per cent in hotels and restaurants, but generally amounted to less than 1 per cent of employees in most industries. Temporary, full-time employees with variable hours constituted 2 per cent of employees overall, exceeding 5 per cent in oil and gas but otherwise 4 per cent or less; several industries had under 1 per cent of their employees on this basis.

The form of flexible employment that combined all three facets of flexibility examined here – part-time, temporary work on variable hours – was one of the least prevalent. Only 2 per cent of employees worked on such a basis. Unsurprisingly, 'hotels and restaurants' and 'education' used this type of employee most commonly, both with 6 per cent. Virtually all other industries

Table 2.2   Combinations of forms of flexible labour by industry, Spring 1994
(labour forms as percentage of total employment)

Row percentages

Industry	Part-time, perm, variable weekly hours	Full-time, temp, fixed weekly hours	Part-time, temp, fixed weekly hours	Full-time, temp, variable weekly hours	Part-time, temp, variable weekly hours	Full-time, perm, variable weekly hours	Part-time, perm, fixed weekly hours	Full-time, perm, fixed weekly hours
			Flexible forms (mutually exclusive)					
Agriculture	10.9	1.6	1.2	2.8	2.1	53.1	6.3	22.0
Oil & gas extraction	1.7	1.8	*	7.2	*	61.5	1.5	26.4
Other mining	1.2	2.7	1.1	4.4	*	51.2	1.1	38.4
Food, drink & tobacco	4.5	0.9	*	1.4	0.7	51.1	7.1	33.8
Textiles	3.1	0.5	*	0.9	0.5	37.2	7.2	50.3
Leather	5.1	1.0	*	*	0.6	32.6	10.4	50.3
Wood products	3.1	2.0	0.6	0.6	0.5	45.6	3.7	43.8
Paper, printing & publishing	4.2	1.3	0.9	1.0	1.5	53.1	5.7	32.3
Oil refining & fuels	3.8	3.8	*	2.8	*	56.7	*	32.9
Chemicals	1.7	2.5	*	3.2	*	53.8	2.6	35.7
Rubber & plastic	3.1	*	0.5	1.3	0.8	53.8	4.1	36.1
Other mineral products	1.8	0.6	*	1.5	*	54.1	2.3	39.3
Metal products & metals	2.0	1.0	*	1.1	*	55.8	3.3	36.6
Machinery & equipment	1.6	1.4	*	1.8	*	57.0	3.5	34.2
Electrical equipment	2.1	1.4	*	2.4	0.6	53.8	3.4	35.7

continued

Table 2.2   continued

Row percentages

	Flexible forms (not mutually exclusive)							
	Part-time, perm, variable weekly hours	Full-time, temp, fixed weekly hours	Part-time, temp, fixed weekly hours	Full-time, temp, variable weekly hours	Part-time, temp, variable weekly hours	Full-time, perm, variable weekly hours	Part-time, perm, fixed weekly hours	Full-time, perm, fixed weekly hours
Transport equipment	0.7	1.4	*	1.9	*	52.9	1.6	41.1
Other manufacturing	3.5	1.3	*	1.1	*	50.0	3.6	40.1
Electricity, gas & water	2.6	2.9	0.6	1.6	0.5	61.1	2.3	28.4
Construction	3.3	2.8	*	2.6	0.7	50.9	3.8	35.8
Distribution	16.0	0.5	1.3	0.6	1.7	30.3	21.3	28.4
Hotels & restaurants	23.9	0.7	2.6	1.4	6.0	26.1	21.9	17.5
Transport & communication	3.7	1.1	0.7	1.9	0.9	60.2	4.5	27.0
Financial services	5.5	1.2	0.6	0.8	0.8	49.5	7.6	33.9
Business services	8.4	2.0	0.8	2.9	1.4	44.8	12.0	27.7
Public administration	5.0	1.8	0.9	2.0	1.2	54.1	6.9	28.2
Education	7.2	1.7	4.6	3.6	5.9	39.1	19.2	18.7
Health & social work	19.0	1.5	1.3	2.6	1.8	28.4	24.0	21.3
Other services	14.2	1.8	2.7	3.3	3.7	33.8	18.7	21.9
All industries[a]	9.4	1.4	1.3	2.0	1.9	42.9	12.9	28.3

* = less than 0.5 per cent
[a] excludes unclassifiable cases

Source: Spring 1994 LFS

used around 1 per cent or less; nine industries used 0.5 per cent or less.

Several industries stand out from this analysis as having distinctive use of these seven forms of flexible labour. 'Hotels and restaurants' was the most distinctive industry, employing the highest proportions of two of the seven forms (part-time, permanent, variable hours; and part-time, temporary, variable hours) and second highest of another (part-time, permanent, fixed hours); it also had the lowest use of full-time, permanent, variable hours employees. 'Oil and gas extraction' was also distinctive in having the highest incidence of two forms (full-time, permanent, variable hours; and full-time, temporary, variable hours), but also the lowest (zero per cent) on two others (part-time, temporary, fixed hours; and part-time, temporary, variable hours). These two contrasting industries highlight differences in employment practice that arise from different technological, industrial and economic conditions that predispose employers to employ different types of labour, often with extremely high concentrations of either men or women.

The occupations involved in flexible employment

Some of the differences in the extent to which employers employ people on different contractual and working-time bases may be thought of as arising from the different types of occupation employed. Occupations are not spread evenly across industries; some are highly industry-specific, others occurring across a wide range of industries. Official coding systems for classifying occupations have changed over the period embraced by the LFS analysis reported here. The classification used in our analysis is one that would allow comparability over the period and is the Registrar General's classification of socio-economic groups. Table 2.3 shows how the three main forms of flexible labour, from the employers' point of view, occurred among employees in each socio-economic group in Spring 1994. For ease of reference we refer to the different categories as occupations, although it is clear that they are broad groupings of occupations.

Table 2.3   Incidence of flexible forms of labour by socio-economic
group, Spring 1994
(labour form as percentage of total employment)

Row percentages

| | Flexible forms (not mutually exclusive) | | |
	Part-time employees	Temporary employees	Variable hours workers
Socio-economic group			
Employers & managers (large establishments)	4.8	2.3	70.0
Employers & managers (small establishments)	10.9	2.0	65.8
Professional workers	6.4	11.1	73.4
Intermediate non-manual	23.9	8.5	59.0
Junior non-manual	43.5	6.8	45.9
Personal service workers	61.2	12.2	47.2
Foremen/supervisors (manual)	7.4	2.7	62.8
Skilled manual	6.0	4.4	60.0
Semi-skilled manual	22.3	7.4	51.5
Unskilled manual	64.2	9.1	34.2
Farm managers	9.9	4.6	80.7
Agricultural workers	20.2	9.5	64.9
Military personnel	4.1	4.0	78.8
Occupations inadequately described	21.7	8.8	51.4
All groups	25.4	6.5	56.3

Source: Spring 1994 LFS

The biggest differences between occupations were in the incidence of *part-time working*. Only 4 per cent of military personnel and 5 per cent of employers and managers in large establishments worked part-time, whereas 61 per cent in personal service occupations and 64 per cent of unskilled manual workers did so. Many of these differences reflect the gender composition of the occupations involved.

The use of *temporary employees* also varied considerably across occupations. It was lowest for employers and managers at 2 per cent and highest for professional and personal service workers, at 11 and 12 per cent respectively. Otherwise occupations contained between 4 and 10 per cent of temporary employees.

Employees whose *hours of work vary* constituted between 50 and 70 per cent of employees in most occupations. Only professional workers and military personnel were above 70 per cent. Junior non-manual and unskilled manual workers were the least likely to work variable hours (45 and 34 per cent respectively). The higher levels of varying hours working among more senior white collar workers fits the conventional perception of their jobs and the requirement to finish tasks or take responsibility for outcomes which they are expected to meet.

Seasonal fluctuations

As the ELUS research and some of its precursors showed, one of the reasons why employers use particular types of flexible labour is to cope with seasonal variations in demand while minimising employment costs. This is most evidently a reason for using temporary employees of any sort. Some businesses have seasonal variations in demand that are so extreme that they may hire substantial numbers of temporary employees at some times of the year and none at all at other times. Many tourism and leisure-related businesses are of this type; agriculture is another example. Other forms of flexible employment may be affected by seasonal factors, besides temporary employees. The fact that the LFS is based upon separate quarterly samples, and that the reference weeks (or other period) for most questions will be similarly distributed, means that some (but certainly not all) of this seasonal pattern may be seen be examining the separate quarterly data.

Table 2.4 shows the results of doing this for the last three quarters of 1993 and the first quarter of 1994, for each of the three main broad categories of 'flexible' employee: part-time workers, temporary workers and those whose hours vary from week to week. For each of these categories the table shows the average percentage of employees over the 12-month period and, in the second column, the degree to which this percentage changed from the lowest quarter (the trough) to the highest quarter (the peak);[6] the result is itself presented as a percentage.[7] Thus, for the economy as a whole, part-time workers formed 25 per cent of employees over the 12-month period and in the peak quarter the proportion was 4 per cent higher than in the trough quarter. The actual quarterly figures were 24.6 per cent in the trough quarter and 25.4 per cent in the peak quarter. A figure of 100 per cent or more in this column means that the percentage of employees working part-time doubled, or more than doubled, from the trough quarter to the peak quarter.

In the economy as a whole it is clear, as expected, that the employment of temporary workers showed greater seasonal variation than the employment of part-time employees (4.9 per cent, compared with 3.5 per cent). Employees with variable hours showed the least amount of seasonality (1.5 per cent), reflecting their capacity to provide seasonally varying labour inputs by changing the extent of variation in hours rather than by moving from having fixed to varying hours.

These aggregate figures for the economy as a whole obscure the amount of variation within individual industries, partly because peaks in one industry correspond with troughs in others. Of course, particular employers or establishments will show even greater variability than whole industries, but even disaggregating the figures to the 28 industries shown in Table 2.4 gives a better impression of the amount of change from one quarter to another. In the typical (median) industry the proportion of employees working on a *part-time* basis increased by 19 per cent from the trough quarter to the peak quarter. Again, as expected, the category with the highest median variability was *temporary workers,* with peak quarters typically employing 32 per cent more workers than trough quarters. Employees with *variable hours* again showed the least amount of seasonal variation, typically 5 per cent from trough to peak.

Looking at the separate industries shown in Table 2.4 the use of *part-time* workers fluctuated during the year to widely differing degrees. In four industries – oil and gas extraction, other mining, oil refining and fuels and other manufacturing – the share of part-time workers doubled, or more than doubled, between the trough quarter and the peak quarter. However, all but the last of these industries was a very low user of part-time workers, even at the peak quarter. On the other hand, there are eight industries where the observed fluctuation through the year was less than 10 per cent. These industries are made up almost

Table 2.4 The degree of variation across the four quarters of the year in the use of the three main categories of flexible labour, 1993–1994

Percentages

| | Flexible forms (not mutually exclusive) | | | | | |
| | Part-time employees | | Temporary employees | | Variable hours workers | |
Industry	Average use	Variation	Average use	Variation	Average use	Variation
Agriculture	22.2	14.1	9.9	80.3	70.7	12.4
Oil & gas extraction	2.4	136.4	11.2	52.6	63.7	17.2
Other mining	2.6	269.9	11.2	72.7	55.5	8.1
Food, drink & tobacco	13.8	25.4	5.3	96.8	58.9	4.1
Textiles	12.6	26.1	2.6	13.1	41.5	2.2
Leather	14.6	18.7	2.6	(high)[a]	48.8	46.0
Wood products	6.3	52.0	2.6	56.1	53.9	10.3
Paper, printing & publishing	13.1	10.3	4.6	9.0	59.7	4.0
Oil refining & fuels	3.2	109.8	6.9	85.0	62.9	6.2
Chemicals	5.7	31.2	4.6	72.1	58.9	5.6
Rubber & plastic	8.5	6.0	3.5	47.4	55.7	8.9
Other mineral products	5.3	26.4	2.9	28.3	57.5	1.4
Metal products & metals	5.9	21.9	2.9	62.6	56.9	6.5
Machinery & equipment	6.1	19.1	3.9	62.9	59.9	0.9
Electrical equipment	5.8	27.6	4.9	12.4	58.6	2.2
Transport equipment	3.2	40.8	3.6	17.3	56.3	3.3
Other manufacturing	10.8	107.8	3.9	113.0	50.3	19.4

continued

Table 2.4 continued

Percentages

| | Flexible forms (not mutually exclusive) | | | | | |
| | Part-time employees | | Temporary employees | | Variable hours workers | |
	Average use	Variation	Average use	Variation	Average use	Variation
Electricity, gas & water	6.7	26.0	4.9	33.8	62.9	13.1
Construction	7.8	8.5	7.2	29.6	56.9	4.4
Distribution	39.7	1.3	4.6	26.9	48.3	1.6
Hotels & restaurants	54.6	3.5	12.1	28.2	55.5	5.5
Transport & communication	9.8	5.3	4.9	13.0	66.5	2.8
Financial services	13.8	9.2	3.6	11.5	56.0	4.7
Business services	19.5	35.2	7.1	5.8	57.8	4.1
Public administration	13.9	9.5	5.5	16.6	61.8	1.3
Education	36.8	3.5	14.8	18.0	54.4	4.5
Health & social work	44.5	8.5	7.3	5.5	50.9	3.2
Other services	41.2	18.0	9.9	29.1	54.1	5.4
All industries[b]	25.0	3.5	6.6	4.9	55.7	1.5
Median variation		18.5		31.6		4.6

* Variation = (share in maximum quarter minus share in minimum quarter) x 100 / share in minimum quarter

[a] Proportion in minimum quarter was less than 0.5 per cent.
[b] Excludes unclassifiable cases.

Source: Summer, Autumn and Winter 1993 and Spring 1994 LFS

equally of those where the proportion of part-time workers in the labour force was high and those where it was low.

In twelve industries the relative use of *temporary workers* changed by 50 per cent or more over the year, and again these industries comprise both high users of temporary workers and low users. The ten industries in which the usage of temporary workers fluctuated by less than 20 per cent are, with the exception of the education sector, all industries in which the use of temporary workers was average or below average.

The industries with a higher than average degree of seasonality in their use of *variable hours* workers generally employed higher than average proportions of this type of worker: agriculture, oil and gas extraction and other manufacturing fit this pattern. The first two mentioned are ones with obvious dependence upon weather conditions; other manufacturing includes the manufacture of toys and sports equipment — products which have strong seasonal patterns of product demand.

Looking across the three categories of flexible labour, industries with seasonal variation higher than typical in all three categories are all extractive or manufacturing industries. There are five of them: agriculture, oil and gas extraction, other mining, wood products and other manufacturing. By contrast there are four industries, all in the service sector, which have lower than typical seasonality in each of the three types of 'flexible' employee. These are distribution, transport and communication, public administration and health and social work; they are readily recognised as parts of the economy with generally stable demand over the course of the year.

Change over time

Employers' use of flexible forms of labour has grown over the last decade on the evidence of the Labour Force Surveys. Growth in the use of part-time, temporary and variable hours workers has been substantial, as shown in Table 2.5. The only form showing no growth between 1984 and 1994 was agency workers, whose share of employment was less than 0.5 per cent of employees in both years. The share of 'new' subcontractors in the workforce[8] grew most rapidly, by 200 per cent, but from a low base (from about 0.1 per cent to 0.3 per cent over the period). The rest of this section examines the change by industry. However, the small number of agency workers and 'new' subcontractors (and, for 'new' subcontractors, the limitations of the variable referred to earlier) meant that analysis by industry could not be justified for these groups. Our analysis therefore concentrates on the main forms of flexible labour, part-time, temporary and variable hours workers.

Table 2.5 shows changes in the incidence of these three main forms of flexibility by industrial sector over the ten-year period, 1984 to 1994. Each of the three forms showed substantial growth.

The form with the highest rate of growth was that involving employees working varying weekly hours of work: the proportion of employees working in this way grew by 87 per cent between 1984 and 1994. The use of workers employed on a temporary basis increased by 53 per cent and the use of workers employed on a part-time basis rose by 25 per cent.

All industries experienced a growth in the proportion of employees whose *hours of work vary*. Moreover, the extent to which the growth was faster in some industries than in others was not large, when compared with the inter-industry differences in growth rates with respect to other forms of flexible labour. The lowest rate of increase was in hotels and restaurants, where it was 24 per cent. Food, drink and tobacco manufacture and oil and gas extraction showed the highest rates of increase, 165 and 143 per cent respectively. Although the industries showing the highest growth were all in the 'production' sector, there appeared to be no overall difference between 'production' and the rest of the economy. Nor was there any association between high incidence in 1984 and low or high growth over the succeeding ten years. The changes in the use of employees with variable hours appear to arise from a widespread set of factors, but without more information about the detailed types of variable hours arrangement it is difficult to give much in the way of explanation.[9] Clearly, changes in the use and amounts of overtime, either paid or unpaid, must be a substantial part of the explanation, since this is probably the major component of the category of workers whose hours varied from week to week.

Table 2.5   Changes in the incidence of use of flexible forms of labour, 1984–1994
(labour form as percentage of total employment)

Percentages

| | Flexible forms (not mutually exclusive) | | | | | |
| | Part-time employees | | Temporary employees | | Variable hours workers | |
Industry	Incidence 1984	% change 1984–94	Incidence 1984	% change 1984–94	Incidence 1984	% change 1984–94
Agriculture	19.4	6.8	9.8	-22.1	44.7	53.8
Oil & gas extraction	1.7	82.8	8.1	9.8	28.9	143.2
Other mining	0.8	303.3	0.2	4369.4	31.5	78.9
Food, drink & tobacco	14.5	-12.1	3.2	4.1	21.9	164.9
Textiles	16.4	-32.0	2.2	1.2	22.1	90.1
Leather	19.8	-18.5	4.9	-67.7	25.7	49.0
Wood products	7.5	3.5	2.4	55.9	34.9	47.2
Paper, printing & publishing	12.0	3.0	3.1	52.0	29.1	106.0
Oil refining & fuels	4.2	-8.7	3.7	76.8	35.1	80.4
Chemicals	6.8	-26.8	2.6	135.3	28.6	106.6
Rubber & plastic	13.3	-35.8	3.3	-8.4	34.1	73.4
Other mineral products	6.0	-24.9	2.5	1.1	26.2	121.0
Metal products & metals	5.2	5.7	1.7	32.7	30.3	94.2
Machinery & equipment	3.6	53.7	1.7	117.6	30.4	99.3
Electrical equipment	5.8	15.9	2.2	113.0	26.0	126.9
Transport equipment	2.5	6.2	1.0	274.7	28.3	96.9

continued

Table 2.5   continued

Percentages

Flexible forms (not mutually exclusive)

	Part-time employees Incidence 1984	Part-time employees % change 1984–94	Temporary employees Incidence 1984	Temporary employees % change 1984–94	Variable hours workers Incidence 1984	Variable hours workers % change 1984–94
Other manufacturing	9.3	-20.5	4.0	-32.7	31.6	73.6
Electricity, gas & water	5.8	1.4	2.4	134.3	28.8	128.5
Construction	6.7	18.5	4.9	27.2	25.6	127.4
Distribution	29.2	36.7	3.0	30.9	27.1	79.4
Hotels & restaurants	57.2	-5.4	9.7	10.2	46.4	23.6
Transport & communication	5.6	79.1	2.1	116.2	33.4	99.8
Financial services	11.2	29.1	1.6	113.4	34.0	66.6
Business services	16.9	33.5	5.4	32.9	36.0	60.7
Public administration	10.6	32.0	3.5	66.6	29.4	111.7
Education	35.3	4.4	10.1	57.1	29.3	90.8
Health & social work	39.8	16.2	4.4	66.4	24.6	111.2
Other services	44.0	-10.7	7.6	51.8	26.7	110.1
All industries[a]	20.4	24.5	4.3	52.9	30.2	86.6

[a] Excludes unclassifiable cases.

Source: Spring 1984 and Spring 1994 LFS

Regarding *part-time employees,* although there was growth in the economy as a whole, not all industries showed an increase over the ten-year period. Indeed, in some industrial sectors there was a distinct fall in the relative use of part-time workers: food drink and tobacco, textiles, leather, oil refining and fuels, chemicals, rubber and plastics, other mineral products, other manufacturing and personal and community services all show falls of at least 10 per cent in the proportion of their employees who worked part-time. On the other hand, some industries showed very substantial gains, but mostly from a very low base. The industry having the most impact on the overall increase was probably distribution, which had a relatively high proportion of part-timers in 1984 and increased that proportion by 37 per cent over the ten-year period.

With respect to *temporary workers,* all but four industries increased the proportion of workers employed in this way. Agriculture was noteworthy, with a higher than average use in 1984 of some 10 per cent and a decline of 20 per cent over the period 1984 to 1994. Industries with a relatively high (in 1984) and growing proportion of temporary workers were hotels and restaurants (growing by 10 per cent), business services (by 33 per cent), education (by 57 per cent) and other services (by 52 per cent).

Looking at all three types of flexible employment across industries, there is no single industry which showed an above average rate of growth for all three types. Nor, on the other hand, was there an industry with below average growth of all three types. The nearest to this is 'other mineral products' which was only marginally below average in its increasing use of variable hours workers.

The general conclusion from Table 2.5 is that, despite the overall increases in the use of all three main types of flexible labour, industries showed different patterns of changing usage for the three types. Generally, large increases in the use of one type were offset by smaller increases (or decreases) in the others.

Changes in the level of part-time, temporary and variable hours working over the period 1984–94 were also examined to see if they were attributable to a growth (or decline) in the importance of industries in terms of employment. This was done using the technique of 'shift-share analysis', which separates the effect of the changing share of each industry's employment within the total from the changing usage of the specified employment form within each industry. The results of this analysis are given in Table 2.6. The table shows the percentage of the total change attributable to each effect.

Table 2.6   Shift-share analysis of changes in use of three main forms of flexible labour

Row percentages

| | *Percentage change in use due to* | | |
	Change in employment across industries	Change in practice within industries	Interaction
Part-time employees	36	48	18
Temporary employees	6	95	0
Variable hours workers	-6	115	-9

| | *Percentage change in use due to* | | |
	Change in employment across occupations	Change in practice within industries	Interaction
Part-time employees	-7	106	1
Temporary employees	-4	103	1
Variable hours workers	3	97	0

The results of this 'shift-share' analysis are quite clear. Changes in employers' practice seem to be the dominant cause of the growth in all three forms of flexible labour, this being particularly true with respect to temporary working and the varying of weekly working hours. Only in the case of part-time working did the expansion of industrial sectors with high usage contribute to the overall increase in the economy.

In relation to occupations the results are even more clear-cut. The changing occupational composition of the economy contributed virtually nothing to the growth of the three types of flexible employment; changes in employers' practices and in employees' behaviour within occupations accounted for the great majority of the changes.

Flexible labour in small establishments

It is widely believed that small employing units have greatly increased their share of employment in the past decade or so. In fact it is probably more accurate to see the changing size composition of employing units as one involving the decline of large units. And while large *organisations and enterprises* have come to employ a declining proportion of employees, this does not necessarily lead to or imply declining employment in large workplaces. Employer-based statistics covering the whole economy are not available, either for organisations or workplaces; only the manufacturing sector is covered by a long-standing statistical series.[10] The LFS has included a question to employees about the size of their place of work, in terms of the number of employees.[11] The question distinguishes the sizes of very small workplaces, but groups those of 25 or more employees together. It therefore has limited use in examining whether the changing size composition of the economy has contributed to the changing use of the main forms of flexible labour – temporary contracts, part-time contracts and opportunities to vary weekly hours. The results are given in Table 2.7.

With respect to the use of both part-time and temporary workers, the fastest growth occurred in larger establishments. Indeed, growth was virtually confined to larger establishments. Part-time employees were more common in small establishments in both years, but the proportion increased only slightly, from 34 to 37 per cent, a change of 9 per cent. Larger establishments employed a smaller proportion, but increased more rapidly, by 42 per cent over the same period.

The different rate of growth was even more marked for temporary employees: 3 per cent for small establishments, compared with 99 per cent for larger ones. Small establishments had been the greater users of temporary workers in 1984 and larger establishments caught them up ten years later.

Only with respect to the existence of opportunities to vary weekly hours was there little difference between establishments of different sizes. Small and larger establishments increased their use of employees on these arrangements by similar proportions (77 and 84 per cent respectively).

Table 2.7   Incidence of flexible forms of labour by establishment size

Percentages

	1984	1994	Percentage change
Proportion of employees in temporary jobs			
Establishments with under 25 employees	6.2	6.4	3.3
Establishments with 25 or more employees	3.3	6.6	99.1
All establishments [a]	4.3	6.5	52.9
Proportion working part-time			
Establishments with under 25 employees	34.0	37.2	9.3
Establishments with 25 or more employees	13.6	19.4	42.3
All establishments [a]	20.4	25.4	24.5
Proportion with varying hours			
Establishments with under 25 employees	29.7	52.5	76.7
Establishments with 25 or more employees	31.7	58.3	83.6
All establishments [a]	31.3	56.3	81.3

[a] excludes unclassifiable cases

Source: Spring 1984 and 1994 LFS

Conclusions

This analysis of the Labour Force Surveys has revealed a number of important points that have a bearing upon employers' use of various types of flexible labour:

- A remarkably high proportion of employees do not work a fixed number of hours per week. Rather, their hours vary in some way (and to an unknown extent) from week to week. Varying amounts of either paid or unpaid overtime must be a substantial if not majority element of this proportion. But, whatever the composition of this large category of workers, it is clear that employers gain some 'flexibility' in their utilisation of labour from such arrangements. And they have done so at least since 1984.

- There has been a substantial increase in the incidence of people working in a flexible form over the past decade. This has resulted not so much from the growing importance of industries or occupations where such forms are likely to be found but from a greater preparedness of employers in all industries to organise labour inputs in this way, although growth in the industries where part-time working was already more common did contribute substantially to the growth in part-time employment. What has motivated employers and how they have been able to achieve the changes cannot be readily discerned from the information available in successive Labour Force Surveys.
- The largest increases in the use of flexible labour occurred in larger establishments (those with 25 or more employees). Larger establishments have been catching up small establishments in their use of flexible labour, particularly temporary employees. This runs counter to a widespread belief that the British labour market is becoming increasingly flexible because of a growth of small workplaces.
- There appears to be an association between the form of flexible working and gender.

The concentration of the most noticeable changes in larger establishments is fortuitous for our purposes, since the employers' survey which was selected for further analysis in this research was confined to establishments of this size. This analysis is reported in Chapter 3.

Notes

1 Many homeworkers, about 67 per cent of those identified in the LFS, claim to be dependent employees. Their legal status is unclear, but they are unlikely to be considered as employees by industrial tribunals and courts. Equally, some agency workers have been held by industrial tribunals to be self-employed, despite their protestations to the contrary. See Casey and Creigh, 1988.

2 The reconciliation of the two classifications to produce a consistent series is taken from Walker (1993). Appendix 1 gives the official title for industries abbreviated in the tables in this chapter.

3 The tables in the text contain percentages. The size of the unweighted bases used in calculating these percentages are given in Appendix 2, whereby Table A2.1 refers to Table 2.1 etc.

4   Some of this overtime is paid, some unpaid. There was little difference in the likelihood to be normally working some paid overtime between those who reported their hours varied and those who did not, and the same applied with respect to unpaid overtime. As might be expected, the proportion working overtime, paid or unpaid, was higher amongst those who reported their hours varied amongst those who did not.

5   The interviewer instruction in the LFS defines 'annualised hours' as situations where 'the number of hours an employee has to work are calculated over a full year... Variations in hours are related to seasonal factors or fluctuations in demand for the company's [sic] goods or services.'

6   Shares for each of the four quarters, for each of the three 'flexible' forms of labour described in this section are given in Appendix 2, Tables B.2.4(i), B2.4(ii) and B2.4(iii).

7   The formula used was (highest quarter minus lowest quarter) divided by lowest quarter.

8   This proportion measures new subcontractors as a percentage of the dependent labour force plus new subcontractors.

9   Some revisions to the current LFS questions would be a help in understanding the phenomenon of variable hours working in the future.

10 Central Statistical Office, Business Monitor PA1003.

11 According to the LFS, the proportion of employees working in establishments with fewer than 25 employees stood at 66 per cent in both 1984 and 1994. Between 1984 and 1990 the proportion working in establishments of 25 employees or more is estimated from the Census of Employment to have fallen from 72 to 70 per cent; the average size of workplaces with 25 or more employees also fell, from 109 to 102 (Millward et al., 1992, p16).

Chapter 3

Evidence from Employer Surveys

Evidence about employers' use of flexible labour is available from a number of large-scale, national employer-based surveys. The most comprehensive and useful for this purpose are the *Workplace Industrial Relations Surveys* of 1980, 1984 and 1990; and the *Employers' Labour Use Strategies* survey of 1987. Of these, the latter has already been extensively analysed (McGregor and Sproull, 1991; Hunter et al, 1993) and, since it was ad hoc, there is no potential for comparing its results with those from previous, similar surveys. On the other hand, the WIRS surveys do form part of a series and contain a number of common questions which allow comparisons through time. The two most recent surveys of 1984 and 1990 were selected for further analysis in this project. Besides their recency they also had the advantage of involving a panel sample for studying changes by establishments through time.

The pros and cons of WIRS for analysing flexibility

The *Workplace Industrial Relations Surveys* have a number of major advantages as a source of information about employers' labour use practices. They are large-scale, national surveys based on a representative sample of over 2,000 workplaces. Funded by the Employment Department, the Economic and Social Research Council, the Policy Studies Institute and the Advisory, Conciliation and Arbitration Service, their purpose has been to provide authoritative research data on the structures and practices of employee relations in Britain. They involve face-to-face interviews with managers and worker representatives, the interviews with managers lasting on average one-and-a-half hours and involving extensive data collection of a wide variety of topics. The scope of the surveys is virtually comprehensive, including all sectors of employment, manufacturing and services, both publicly and privately owned. The only significant exclusions are agriculture, coal-mining and very small workplaces. This last exclusion, workplaces having fewer than 25 employees, is a substantial drawback for some research purposes, especially where the phenomena being considered are especially prevalent in small workplaces, as some types of flexible labour are. Nevertheless, the surveys cover a clear majority of employees, approximately 70 per cent of workers in employment in Great Britain. In addition, analysing results by size of workplace can go a good way towards assessing whether the exclusion of small establishments is a major drawback.

A more important disadvantage for current purposes is that the surveys were not designed with a focus on employers' labour use practices. They do, however, contain a number of questions which relate to this topic, although the questioning is generally of little depth and was designed mainly to provide background information for the analysis of industrial relations practices. Whilst these disadvantages have to be accepted for the current secondary analysis project, they are not inherent in large-scale survey research and we will return to the question of how workplace surveys could illuminate the question of employers' labour use practices in our final chapter of this report.

Having stressed that the WIRS surveys were not created with our present purposes in mind, it has to be said that they do have a number of very positive features. First of all, the data are of high quality; both fieldwork and editing were carried out to very high standards. Secondly, each of the surveys was carried out by the same fieldwork organisation (Social and Community Planning Research), so that unknowable measurement errors caused by the use of different organisations to collect and edit the data are largely eliminated. Thirdly, the surveys are highly representative of the population (workplaces with 25 or more employees). They are based on a properly constructed statistical sample with a very high response rate: 77 per cent for the 1984 survey and 83 per cent for the 1990 survey. Fourthly, their coverage of both public and private sectors, manufacturing and services, gives them a high level of generality.

The WIRS data on flexibility

Flexibility is a flexible concept. Our focus here is on employment relationships and types of employment contract that permit the employer to make relatively rapid adjustments in labour supply to variations in product demand, or to acquire the use of specialised competencies for which there is insufficient sustained demand to justify a permanent job. Of course, employers can have a wide variety of reasons for employing different types of labour (McGregor and Sproull, 1991, pp27–29). Most of the reasons given by managers in the ELUS survey were traditional reasons and the newer rationales, such as the avoidance of unionisation and of employment rights, were rarely given. There was no attempt in WIRS to ask about these reasons, since they had been covered in ELUS. In addition, taking the full-time, permanent worker employed on an indefinite employment contract as the benchmark, non-standard employment practices come in a rich variety. Only a small number of them were the subject of questioning in WIRS. In fact, only two types of non-standard worker were asked about in both the 1984 and 1990 surveys. These were:

- employees working on a short fixed-term for 12 months or less;
- individuals paid on a freelance basis or as homeworkers or outworkers (not employees).

Arrangements that were *not* asked about in WIRS 1984 or 1990 include:

- agency temps
- temporary, casual, 'on-call', seasonal or task workers not on a short, fixed-term contract.

Other arrangements or practices that would also be included in most definitions of 'numerical flexibility' and *were* asked about in WIRS are the following:

- part-time employees
- overtime working
- shift-working
- subcontracting of services.

There were also two questions that relate to reductions in labour input. The first of these concerned methods of permanently reducing the workforce such as natural wastage, early retirement, voluntary redundancy and compulsory redundancy. The second concerned the smaller scale and more temporary reductions in labour input, namely short-time working, temporary lay-offs, a reduction in the number of shifts worked, and other work-sharing arrangements. Questioning on temporary or permanent increases in labour input was much more limited: it was confined to a question on whether any recruitment to the establishment's workforce had taken place within the last twelve months. Retrospective questions about the workforce twelve months and three (or four) years ago were also included in both surveys, but they did not distinguish between different types of employee such as full-time, or part-time, let alone any of the types of non-standard employee such as short-term contract workers.

The two main types of non-standard employment that we examine here are the use of short-term contract workers and of freelancers or homeworkers. After describing their incidence in 1990 in relation to the wide variety of workplace characteristics available in WIRS, we compare their use with more conventional forms of numerical flexibility, namely the use of part-time employees and the use of overtime. The questions on short-term contract workers and freelancers or homeworkers were asked in both the 1984 and 1990 surveys in the same way and can thus be used to give a picture at those two points in time and an indication of any changes in use. In a later section we use the 1984/1990 WIRS panel sample to examine the characteristics of workplaces that increased or decreased their use of these two types of employment relationship.

WIRS results for 1990

Short-term contract workers

The actual question addressed to the main WIRS management respondents in both surveys was: 'Are any employees of this establishment currently working on the basis of a short fixed-term contract for twelve months or less?'. Those that responded 'yes' were asked the question 'how many?'. Non-response to both these questions was low in both surveys. On the first question only 1 per cent of respondents were unable to give a definite 'yes or no' answer in 1990. On the numerical question, there was more non-response, amounting to 6 per cent of those answering 'yes' and 1 per cent of the whole sample. However, non-response on the numerical question was high in very large, public sector workplaces where the proportion of short-term contract workers (among those that reported usage) was higher than average. This strongly suggests that respondents were unable to give precise numbers where the numbers were large, and that the results should therefore not be used to produce grossed-up estimates of the numbers of short-term contract workers in the WIRS sample as a whole, let alone the British economy in general in 1990.

Our preferred use of the data is to classify establishments in terms of their *intensity of use of short-term contract workers,* taking account of the size of the establishment's workforce. Eighty per cent of establishments reported using no short-term contract workers in 1990. Of the remaining 20 per cent, 19 out of 20 were able to give numerical estimates of numbers. Of those workplaces with one or more short-term contract workers, the great majority of cases were ones where they formed less than 10 per cent of the workforce. In fact, for those with short-term contract workers the median percentage of short-term contract workers as a proportion of the workforce was 5 per cent. We therefore classified users as 'high' if they had 5 per cent or more of their workforce as short-term contract workers, and as 'low' if the percentage was less than 5 per cent but greater than 0 per cent.

In the sample as a whole, 10 per cent of workplaces were high users, 9 per cent were low users, 80 per cent were non-users, with the remaining 1 per cent unclassifiable because numbers were not reported. Taking cases where the number of short-term contract workers was known, high users employed 80 per cent of this type of worker in the WIRS sample. On average, as shown at the bottom of Table 3.1, short-term contract workers constituted 17 per cent of their employed workforce. Thus, focusing attention on high users means covering the highest concentrations of such workers and the types of workplace where they constituted an important component of the available labour.

Table 3.1 uses the above threefold classification of the use of short-term contract workers to show variation in their use across broad sectors of the economy. Clearly the concentration of high users is in the public services, non-trading sector, where 26 per cent of workplaces were classified as high users. Only just over one half of workplaces in this sector used no short-term contract workers at all, compared with over 90 per cent being non-users in the remainder of the economy. In the trading sector (industry and commerce),[1] only 4 per cent of workplaces were high users, with both manufacturing and services having equal proportions.

The lower panel of Table 3.1 displays a more detailed analysis of the non-trading public services sector. The outstanding sector is school education where 44 per cent of workplaces were high users, 29 per cent were low users and only 26 per cent of cases had no short-term contract workers at all. High users were also common in construction (mostly local authority workplaces) and 'other education' (mostly further education colleges). In medical services 13 per cent of workplaces were high users and 40 per cent low users.

Short-term contract workers in the trading sector

Within industry and commerce relatively few workplaces had a high or even low usage of short-term contract workers. A large number of workplace and employer characteristics were examined in our analysis to detect patterns of high and low usage, but relatively few clear relationships emerged. Table 3.2 summarises results from a number of the more salient characteristics.

Larger workplaces (those having 500 or more employees) appeared to have a higher propensity to use short-term contract workers. They had a higher-than-usual incidence of high use, and a higher-than-usual incidence of low usage; fewer of them had no short-term contract workers at all. In terms of ownership

Table 3.1 Incidence of short-term contract workers, 1990, by broad sector and by industry within the public sector

	Proportion of workplaces where number of short-term contract workers, as a proportion of the whole workforce, was:				
	High (5+%)	Low (1–4%)	Zero	Unweighted base	Weighted base
	Row percentages				
All workplaces	10	9	80	2061	2000
Broad sector					
Public services, non-trading	26	19	53	551	548
Trading sector, of which	4	5	91	1510	1452
Manufacturing	4	3	93	636	427
Services	4	6	90	874	1025
Public services, selected industries (1980 SIC)					
Construction	(39)	(–)	(61)	15	14
Higher education	(8)	(20)	(69)	23	5
Schools	44	29	26	84	202
Other education	(41)	(–)	(59)	20	15
Medical services	13	40	42	135	33
Miscellaneous services	21	17	60	91	119
	Means				
Average percentage of workforce on short fixed-term contracts all workplaces	17	3	0	2011	1991

Figures in brackets are based upon unweighted base of less than 50 and should be treated with caution.
Row percentages may not total to 100 because of rounding or because some workplaces could not be classified.

Table 3.2   Incidence of short-tern contract workers, 1990, within the trading sector by various characteristics

Row percentages

Proportion of workplaces where number of short-term contract workers, as a proportion of the whole workforce, was:

	High (5+%)	Low (1–4%)	Zero	Unweighted base	Weighted base
All trading sector	4	5	91	1510	1452
Establishment size (employees)					
25–99	3	4	92	528	1136
100–499	5	9	86	555	288
500 or more	6	12	80	427	28
Ownership					
Public sector	1	2	97	81	46
Private sector UK	4	5	91	1162	1250
Foreign owned	7	7	86	219	137
Trusts, charities	10	13	77	58	87
Selected industries (1980 SIC)					
Energy and water	12	8	78	52	21
Metal goods manufacture	10	*	90	30	30
Food, drink, tobacco	11	10	79	71	31
Rubber, plastic and other manufacture	10	2	87	37	34
Education	(20)	(11)	(69)	21	36
Medical services	(18)	(–)	(82)	14	30

continued

Table 3.2 continued

Row percentages

	Proportion of workplaces where number of short-term contract workers, as a proportion of the whole workforce, was:				
	High (5+%)	Low (1–4%)	Zero	Unweighted base	Weighted base
Labour costs as proportion of total costs					
Less than 75%	4	5	91	507	606
75% or more	(29)	(19)	(51)	26	17
Trade union representation					
Union(s) recognised	3	5	92	903	584
Members but no recognition	8	4	88	104	134
No members at establishment	3	6	90	489	713
Union membership density (where present)					
1–49%	3	4	93	261	257
50–74%	6	3	90	216	179
75–99	3	5	93	373	180
100%	–	*	100	54	48

1 Figures in brackets are based upon unweighted base of less than 50 and should be treated with caution.
2 Row percentages may not total to 100 because of rounding or because some workplaces could not be classified.

categories, the small publicly-owned part of the trading sector was particularly low in its use of short-term contract workers. In the private sector, foreign-owned companies and trusts and charities had notably higher usage. Industries that appeared to have a higher incidence of high users were energy and water supply, metal goods manufacture, food, drink and tobacco manufacturing, miscellaneous manufacturing, education and medical services. Both these latter two industries were ones where the bulk of the establishments were in the public non-trading sector, where the use of short-term contract workers was particularly high.

A number of economic characteristics of trading sector workplaces were examined, but they showed no clear patterns. The only one that did was the one shown in Table 3.2 which is the labour cost ratio. Here the very small number of workplaces whose cost structure was dominated by labour costs had a much higher usage of short-term contract workers. Unfortunately this variable contains a large number of missing cases in the 1990 WIRS and the relationship is far from being firmly established. There does, however, appear to be a plausible rationale for it, since firms more or less entirely dependent on labour for their valued added would seek to minimise their demand-induced risks in this way. The tabulations also showed a slight tendency for workplaces where labour productivity was assessed by managers as being a lot higher than other establishments in their industry to have a greater use of short-term contract workers. However, since even the high users only had, on average, 17 per cent of their workforce on short-term contracts, it is unlikely that their higher productivity could be attributed to this feature of their labour force. As far as we are aware, none of the recently reported econometric work examining the 1990 WIRS labour productivity variables has included the use of short-term contract workers as an explanatory variable (Moreton, 1995; Fernie and Metcalf, 1995).

A number of features of trade union representation were examined to detect possible relationships with the use of short-term contract workers. Trade unions are often opposed to the idea of replacing permanent jobs with short-term, or contract, jobs, but there was little evidence in the survey data to support the notion that such opposition had been effective. Workplaces with recognised unions were just as likely as other workplaces in the trading sector to have high, low, or no usage, of short-term contract workers. The only hint that this might be despite union opposition was that workplaces without recognised unions, but with union members, had a greater incidence of high usage. A more telling piece of evidence concerns trade union membership density. Although there was no clear pattern across the majority of the range of union densities, the small proportion of workplaces that had 100 per cent membership contained no cases where there were any short-term contract workers. Workplaces with very high density (90–99 per cent) were much less likely to have high usage of short-term contract workers than those with medium and high union membership density. This could be because short-term contract workers were less likely to be union members.[2] Alternatively, it might suggest that the strongest union shops are still predisposed and able to resist the introduction of short-term contract workers. However, we have no information as to whether management had attempted to introduce short-term contract jobs in these cases.

The relationship between the use of short-term contract workers and the more conventional types of numerical flexibility, such as part-time working and overtime, will be discussed in a later section in this chapter.

Freelance workers, homeworkers and outworkers

The second type of non-standard worker asked about in both the 1984 and 1990 WIRS surveys was freelance workers. In contrast to short, fixed-term contract workers discussed above, freelance workers were considered to be an addition to (not part of) the establishment's workforce and, although the question did not specify this, it can be assumed that in the great majority of cases they were not employees of the employer owning the establishment. Rather, freelancers were asked about on the assumption that they were working on a contract for services, not a contract of employment. It should be noted that the employment status of many of these workers is often uncertain, even for those concerned. The actual question about them in WIRS was: 'In the last twelve months, has this establishment paid any individuals on a freelance basis, or as homeworkers, or outworkers?'. The responses coded were: 'Yes, freelance basis', 'Yes, homeworkers/ outworkers', 'Yes, freelancers, homeworkers/

outworkers (no difference between them)' or 'No'. Stating possible responses in this way indicates that the survey designers were aware of variations across different workplaces in the terminology used for similar types of worker. However, there were in fact very few cases where respondents did not distinguish between freelancers, homeworkers and outworkers (less than half of one per cent), and the industrial distribution of the two main types of response suggests that the terms were used to cover workers of different occupational statuses, rather than having a different type of employment relationship.

Homeworkers and outworkers were largely confined to the private sector and, predominantly, to manufacturing industry. They are known from other sources (Hakim, 1985) to be mostly in manual jobs. Freelancers are more often in professional and other white-collar (non-manual) occupations in the services sector. Bearing this in mind, for the rest of this report we refer simply to 'freelancers' as including all three categories of worker.

The follow-up to the WIRS question on the use of any freelancers merely asked for the number of freelance (or home-workers or outworkers) who had carried out work for the sampled establishment in the previous twelve months. The numbers were recorded separately for the two main categories, but in this analysis they have been combined. Note that the question did not distinguish between freelancers who worked more or less continually for the whole of the previous year and those who worked on very brief assignments. The numbers can, therefore, not be considered as in any way comparable to the equivalent numbers of full-time employees. Nevertheless a broad indicator of the relative addition to the workforce can be obtained by dividing the number of freelancers reported by each establishment by that establishment's workforce. Over the whole sample, 83 per cent of workplaces reported employing no freelance workers, and amongst the remaining 17 per cent the median percentage was 6 per cent. Our summary variable of the use of freelancers thus defines three categories of workplace:

- high freelance users (where they amounted to 7 per cent or more of the establishment's workforce)
- low users (1–6 per cent)
- non-users.

This categorisation captures the nature of the highly skewed distribution of freelance workers: 87 per cent of freelancers reported were in the 8 per cent of establishments in the whole sample classified as 'high users'. Among these high users, the average number of freelance workers constituted an addition of 38 per cent of their employee workforce.[3] Among low users, accounting for 9 per cent of the whole sample, the corresponding figure was 3 per cent. Naturally, our classification of workplaces into high and low users, and non-users, omits cases where the numbers of freelance workers were not given. These cases were generally in the types of workplace where numbers, where given, were high or very high. They were most prevalent in the higher education sector of public services, and in larger workplaces in the trading sector. Since these cases are necessarily omitted, it should be borne in mind that the contrasts between high, low and non-users in our analysis are likely to be less than in the population.

Table 3.3 shows the incidence of the three types of establishment according to their use of freelancers across the broad sectors of the economy and, in more detail, within the non-trading public services sector. In contrast to the use of short-term contract workers, the use of freelancers is predominantly a trading sector phenomenon. Ten per cent of trading sector workplaces were high users, compared with 3 per cent in public services; 11 per cent of trading sector workplaces were low users, compared with 5 per cent of public services workplaces. Within the trading sector, manufacturing contained more high and low users than private sector services.

Within the non-trading public services sector, higher education (universities, polytechnics) and other education (that is further education colleges) stood out as the industries with the highest use. Only 32 per cent of higher education establishments, and 53 per cent of other education establishments, reported not using freelancers. In higher education there was a very high degree of non-response to the follow-up question on the number of freelancers. These non-respondents were generally very large employers and are likely to have had large numbers of freelance workers, but which could not be accurately reported without a great deal of effort by respondents. It is likely that most of the workers involved in these cases were occasional lecturing staff.

Table 3.3   Incidence of freelancers, 1990, by broad sector and by industry within the public sector

	Proportion of workplaces where number of freelancers, as a proportion of the whole workforce, was:			Unweighted base	Weighted base
	High (5+%)	Low (1–4%)	Zero		
	Row percentages				
All workplaces	8	9	82	2061	2000
Broad sector					
Public services, non-trading	3	5	91	551	548
Trading sector, of which	10	11	78	1510	1452
Manufacturing	14	15	71	636	427
Services	8	10	82	874	1025
Public services, selected industries (1980 SIC)					
Higher education	(–)	(6)	(32)	23	5
Other education	(28)	(17)	(53)	20	15
Medical services	1	12	87	135	33
Miscellaneous services	9	5	86	91	119
	Means				
Average percentage addition to workforce represented by					
Freelancers	32	3	–	2021	1989
Home/outworkers	9	1	–	2021	1989

Figures in brackets are based upon unweighted base of less than 50 and should be treated with caution.
Row percentages may not total to 100 because of rounding or because some workplaces could not be classified.

Elsewhere in the public services sector, miscellaneous services (covering cemetery and cleaning services, research and development, social welfare, recreational and other cultural services, personal services etc) contained relatively high proportions of high users of freelance workers for the public sector. Medical services contained very few establishments with high usage, but substantial numbers of low users of freelance workers. The remainder of the public sector, essentially central government and local government administration, had a low, or average, incidence of the use of freelance workers.

In the trading sector, freelancers were much more common. Ten per cent of trading sector workplaces were high users, 11 per cent were low users, and only 78 per cent reported using none at all. Table 3.4 shows more detailed results for a number of workplace and employer characteristics which are related to the use of freelance workers. The first of these is establishment size, with smaller workplaces (those with fewer than 100 employees) being substantially more likely to be high users than larger establishments with 500 or more workers. This is in marked contrast to the pattern for short-term contract workers, and supports the notion that freelance workers are used, in part, to carry out work of a short-term, or specialist nature, which is in insufficient demand to occupy a part-time or full-time employee. This interpretation is reinforced by the second panel of the table in which small firms (those having a single establishment) are identified as having substantially greater use of freelance workers than the rest of the trading sector. Other aspects of ownership are shown in the same panel. Again, the public sector (trading) made somewhat lower use of freelance workers than the private sector; and with freelancers there was no difference between foreign-owned and UK-owned private sector workplaces. Trusts, charities and other forms of corporate ownership scored more highly: again this is likely to reflect in part their smaller average size.

The next panel in the table shows industries selected as having generally higher than normal usage of freelancers within the trading sector. In clothing, leather and footwear, some 40 per cent of workplaces were classified as high users, reflecting the widespread use of homeworkers and outworkers in that industry. Other portions of manufacturing industry with relatively high use

Table 3.4   Incidence of freelancers, 1990, within the trading sector by various characteristics

Row percentages

| | Proportion of workplaces where number of freelancers, as a proportion of the whole workforce, was: | | | | |
	High (5+%)	Low (1–4%)	Zero	Unweighted base	Weighted base
All trading sector	10	11	78	1510	1452
Establishment size (employees)					
25–99	11	11	78	528	1136
100–499	7	11	80	555	288
500 or more	3	9	85	427	28
Ownership					
Public sector	8	4	89	81	46
Private sector UK	10	11	78	1162	1250
Foreign owned	9	10	81	219	137
Trusts, charities	28	12	61	58	87
Partnerships, self-proprietorships	15	18	67	70	113
Single establishment firms	14	15	71	239	412
Selected industries (1980 SIC)					
Mechanical engineering	14	27	59	83	64
Electrical engineering	10	26	64	106	50
Leather, footwear, clothing	(40)	(11)	(48)	38	38
Timber, furniture, paper & printing	22	13	65	85	84
Misc. manufacturing	(15)	(26)	(58)	37	34
Construction	19	15	65	57	76
Business services	23	16	61	96	135
Education	(31)	(8)	(61)	21	36

continued

Table 3.4 continued

Row percentages

	Proportion of workplaces where number of freelancers, as a proportion of the whole workforce, was:				Unweighted base	Weighted base
	High (5 +%)	Low (1–4%)	Zero			
Labour costs as proportion of total costs						
Less than 75%	7	8	85		507	606
75% or more	(31)	(1)	(68)		26	17
Age of workplace (years)						
Up to 6	18	14	68		267	316
7–20	12	14	74		375	457
21 or more	5	9	86		829	643
Trade union representation						
Union(s) recognised	5	6	88		903	584
Members but no recognition	27	15	58		104	134
No members at establishment	11	14	75		489	713
Union membership density (where present)						
1–49%	10	12	78		261	257
50–74%	9	10	80		216	179
75–99	4	6	90		373	180
100%	–	1	99		54	48

Figures in brackets are based upon unweighted base of less than 50 and should be treated with caution.
Row percentages may not total to 100 because of rounding or because some workplaces could not be classified.

were mechanical and electrical engineering, timber, furniture, paper and printing and miscellaneous manufacturing industries. In the non-manufacturing sector, construction and business services were high users, and the commercial sections of the education sector (private schools and vocational training) were high users. Workplace size plays little part in explaining why these industries were higher-than-average users. Some of them had a higher proportion of small establishments, but others did not.

A number of economic and product market characteristics of workplaces were examined in the analysis, but the only one with a clear association with the high use of freelance workers was the proportion of total costs accounted for by labour costs. Here the small proportion of workplaces recorded as having a labour cost ratio of 75 per cent or more were much more likely to have a high use of freelancers. Freelancers appeared to be somewhat less common in workplaces with falling output or demand, and more common among those that supplied a large proportion of their output to a single customer. However, those supplying 70 per cent or more of their output to their largest customer had lower usage of freelance workers.

There was a clear relationship with the age of workplaces. Younger workplaces (less than 6 years old) were substantially more likely to use freelance workers than older workplaces, particularly those over 20 years old. This is likely to be partly a function of differences in size, industrial activity, unionisation and so on. The oldest workplaces were substantially larger than average, but younger and medium-aged workplaces were very similar in size, so the higher use of freelance workers among younger establishments is clearly not just a size effect.

Finally, Table 3.4 gives the results for two aspects of trade union representation. From the first panel we see that workplaces with recognised trade unions were substantially less likely to use freelancers than workplaces without recognised unions. However, amongst the latter, those with members but no recognition for wage bargaining were the most likely to use freelancers; they were also particularly likely to be high users. These workplaces with union members but no recognition were generally larger than those with no union members, so the difference between the two cannot be explained, even in part, as a size effect. The results suggest that trade union opposition to the use of freelance workers may be effective where they are sufficiently strong to have recognition for bargaining purposes, but ineffective where such recognition is absent. The results in the final panel of Table 3.4 also point towards this conclusion. In workplaces in the trading sector where union membership was 100 per cent, freelance workers were virtually absent; and the overall relationship between union density and the use of freelancers was progressively negative.

Whilst these cross-sectional results cannot determine the direction of causality, it seems likely that the relative absence of freelancers in highly unionised workplaces either indicates that the most powerful union workplace organisations are able to resist the employment of freelance workers, or (less plausibly) that a high usage of freelance workers undermines trade union organisation amongst employees at the workplace. This is an issue that we will address when examining results obtained from the WIRS panel sample, later in this chapter.

The two types of 'non-standard labour'

The above discussion of the two types of non-standard labour covered by WIRS has indicated that they are associated with different sets of workplace and employer characteristics. In fact, the two types are so distinct that there is no overall correlation between their use. Only 1 per cent of workplaces were high users of both short-term contract workers and freelancers. Only 4 per cent used any of both types. Users of one type but not the other were more or less evenly split between those that used short-term contract workers but not freelancers (17 per cent of workplaces) and those that did the opposite (15 per cent). Workplaces that used none of both types amounted to 66 per cent of the sample. This reinforces the conclusion drawn from the ELUS research programme that the different types of non-standard labour have different underlying rationales and are not usefully lumped together (Hunter et al, 1993). It is also clear that different factors will affect their incidence through time.

Non-standard labour and traditional forms of labour flexibility

How does employers' use of the two types of non-standard labour examined here relate to more traditional categories of 'flexible labour' and other indicators of variable or changing labour requirements? We address this question in two parts. First, by looking at the incidence of the two types in relation to traditional forms of flexibility for which there are WIRS data: part-time working and overtime working. Second, we look at a number of other indicators of variable or changing labour demand.

Although its relative incidence has undoubtedly increased in recent years, *part-time working* has always been a feature of the British labour market and it has always been concentrated among women and in certain industry sectors. The incidence of part-time employment *within workplaces* was first examined using a nationally representative sample of British workplaces by Blanchflower and Corry (1987) using the 1980 WIRS. Using cross-tabular and regression methods they identified the following characteristics as being associated with the (relatively high) use of part-timers: non-manufacturing, larger workplace size (but peaking at around 1,500 employees), the use of short-term contract and freelance workers, private sector, being part of a multi-establishment organisation, lack of formal industrial relations procedures and the presence of a non-manual (but not a manual) closed shop. Surprisingly, the proportion of the work-force that was female was not included. Moreover, Blanchflower and Corry's dependent variable, being a 'part-time using establishment', was defined using a mixture of absolute and proportionate measures. This is undesirable and we have not replicated their definition in our current analysis. Instead, we follow our previous practice in this chapter with regard to the use of non-standard labour and define three categories of use: high, low and none. High and low users are split around the approximate median of proportionate use by users, which in the case of part-timers is 14 per cent of employees. Thus 41 per cent of workplaces (having 14 per cent or more of their current workforce working 30 hours or less) were classified as 'high' users of part-time employees; 42 per cent were low users; and 16 per cent used no part-timers.[4]

High use of part-time employees in 1990, using this classification of workplaces, was associated with: the public sector, non-manufacturing, a high proportion of females, a high proportion of non-manual employees, smaller workplace size (below 100 employees), fewer ethnic minority workers, and a high labour cost ratio (over 50 per cent of total costs).

The second traditional form of numerical flexibility examined here is the use of overtime. Although overtime hours have been reported in both the 1984 and 1990 WIRS, these have never been used to define an establishment-level variable in any published analysis of which we are aware. We have done so in this research because of the centrality of overtime working to employers' flexible use of labour.

The WIRS data are not ideal because they only refer to five out of the eight occupational groups into which the whole of a workplace's employees are categorised. While they omit professional, technical and most sales-related employees, who are more likely to work unpaid overtime hours (Watson, 1992), they do cover the majority of non-managerial employees. The source data come from a question following on from a question about the typical pay of: unskilled manual; semi-skilled manual; skilled manual; clerical, administrative or secretarial; and supervisory employees. We have classified the employees in each of these five groups as working overtime (in the last pay period) if the total weekly hours of the typically-paid worker exceeded 41 (or 39 in the case of clericals). This is designed to capture unpaid as well as paid overtime and also to exclude small amounts of overtime by setting the threshold just above the usual standard working week for most employees. The variable sums the number of employees working overtime and divides by the total number of employees in the five groups present at the workplace.

On this basis, workplaces can be divided into 'high' overtime users, where all the workers covered by the questions (and present) worked overtime, 'low' users, where only some of them worked overtime, and non-users. Eleven per cent of workplaces in the whole sample were unclassifiable because of missing data. Of the remainder, 15 per cent were 'high' overtime users, 12 per cent 'low' and 73 per cent were non-users.

High overtime users tended to be establishments which were: in the private sector, manufacturing, small firms, male-dominated, employing predominantly manual workers, employing no or few part-timers, working at full capacity, and having high manual trade union membership density. These characteristics are generally the opposite of those associated with high part-time usage. Indeed, the expected negative association with part-time usage was strong. Non-users of part-time employees were three times more likely to be high overtime users than high part-time users (25 per cent compared with 8 per cent). Only 3 per cent of the WIRS sample were both high part-time users and high overtime users.

With these characteristics in mind, we examined the use of non-standard employment (short-term contracts and freelance work) in relation to the two traditional forms of flexibility, part-time work and overtime working. The two types of non-standard employment showed different patterns. *Short-term contract work* was positively associated with part-time working; high users of part-time employees were much more likely (three times) to be high users of short-term contract workers than either low part-time users or non-users of part-timers (Table 3.5). Conversely, high use of short-term contract workers was negatively associated with overtime use. There were virtually no workplaces that were high users of short-term contracts and overtime. The employment of *freelancers,* however, showed no clear associations with either part-time working or overtime working (Table 3.6).

We turn, then, to other indicators of changing labour requirements to see whether these are associated with the use of non-standard labour. The first we examined was the overall change in the size of the workforce, not a true indicator of changing labour demand, but a reasonable proxy – assuming that the required adjustments were made over a relatively short period. Similar patterns were evident whether we chose change over the preceeding year, 3 years or 6 years. Workplaces with stable workforce size were more likely to employ high numbers of short-term contract workers than workplaces that had either expanded or contracted (Table 3.5). This largely reflects the greater stability of workforce size (and most employment) in the public services sector, where short-term contract workers are more prevalent. While there was very little association with the occurrence of recent workforce reductions, there was a strong association with recent reductions brought about by the subcontracting of work (although the number of such cases was small) and, to a lesser extent, with reductions due to budget restrictions. Again these were largely a public sector pheno-menon. As to methods of reducing the workforce, high users of short-term contract workers tended towards the use of early retirement and voluntary redundancies. However, the few cases where management reported workforce reductions brought about by terminating the employment of temporary or casual workers were almost entirely confined to high users of short-term contract workers. This suggests that the rationale for employing short-term contract workers is indeed their 'disposibility'. Another such indication was given by the higher use of short-term contract workers in trading sector workplaces which had resorted to temporay lay-offs in the past year. Moreover, trading sector workplaces that were high users of short-term contract workers had a substantially higher rate of dismissal (for reasons other than redundancy) than other workplaces (Table 3.5) – another indication of 'hire and fire' management.

Besides the various indicators of 'numerical flexibility' discussed above, the 1990 WIRS contained questions about the flexibility available to management in the way it organised work. The initial question asked whether management was able to organise work as it wished, or if there were limits to the way it could organise work. Respondents indicating that management faced constraints were asked what those constraints were. The initial overview of these results (Millward et al., 1992, pp329–333) made clear that constraints, whether emanating from trade unions, employees or management, were much more common in public sector workplaces. Naturally, then, there was an association between such constraints and the use of short-term contract workers in the sample as a whole. However, within the individual sectors (trading and public sector non-trading) there was no obvious association. The only specific association of any note was that in the public services sector managers in workplaces with a high use of short-term contract workers were more likely to cite 'lack of skills among the workforce' as a constraint. But only a third of public sector managers citing this difficulty were in workplaces with a 'high' use of short-term contract workers, defined in our analysis as having at least 5 per cent of employees working under such conditions. This suggests that hiring short-term contract workers is not a widespread managerial response to skill shortages in the public sector or, indeed, in the private sector, either manufacturing or services.

Table 3.5   Use of short-term contract workers in relation to other indicators of flexibility, 1990

| | Proportion of workplaces where number of short-term contract workers, as a proportion of the whole workforce, was: | | | | |
	High (5+%)	Low (1–4%)	Zero	Unweighted base	Weighted base
			Row percentages		
All workplaces	10	9	80	2061	2000
Use of part-time employees					
High	17	14	68	660	835
Low	4	6	90	861	818
None	6	5	88	487	325
Use of overtime among 5 occupational groups					
High	2	3	95	207	275
Low	5	7	87	341	206
None	11	9	79	1284	1303
Change in workforce in last 6 years					
Decreased 20% or more	8	10	80	220	135
Decreased 5–20%	8	19	73	198	200
Stable	18	8	74	198	216
Increased 5–20%	11	9	79	187	210
Increased 20% or more	7	9	84	388	476
Workforce reductions in last 12 months					
Yes	12	11	77	917	639
No	9	9	82	1127	1346

continued

Table 3.5 continued

| | Proportion of workplaces where number of freelancers, as a proportion of the whole workforce, was: | | | | |
	High (5+%)	Low (1–4%)	Zero	*Unweighted base*	*Weighted base*
			Row percentages		
Reasons for workforce reductions					
Budget reductions/cash limits	17	11	72	*180*	*115*
Subcontracting of work	(40)	(1)	(59)	*25*	*15*
Method used to reduce workforce					
Early retirement	18	22	60	*464*	*166*
Voluntary redundancies	15	11	74	*369*	*134*
Termination of temp. employment	(96)	(–)	4	*11*	*12*
			Means		
Dismissals per thousand employees					
Public services sector	3	2	4	*513*	*541*
Trading sector	27	11	20	*1498*	*1448*
			Row percentages		
Any recruitment in last year					
Yes	9	10	81	*1923*	*1780*
No	17	6	76	*121*	*200*

Figures in brackets are based upon unweighted base of less than 50 and should be treated with caution.
Row percentages may not total to 100 because of rounding or because some workplaces could not be classified.

Table 3.6   Use of freelancers in relation to other indicators of flexibility, 1990

| | Proportion of workplaces where number of freelancers, as a proportion of the whole workforce, was: | | | | |
	High (5+%)	Low (1–4%)	Zero	Unweighted base	Weighted base
	Row percentages				
All workplaces	8	9	82	2061	2000
Use of part-time employees					
High	6	7	87	660	835
Low	11	12	76	861	818
None	5	10	84	487	325
Use of overtime among 5 occupational groups					
High	10	8	82	207	275
Low	7	18	75	341	206
None	8	9	83	1284	1303
Workforce reductions in last 12 months					
Yes	9	10	81	917	639
No	8	9	82	1127	1346

continued

Table 3.6   continued

| | Proportion of workplaces where number of freelancers, as a proportion of the whole workforce, was: | | | | |
	High (5+%)	Low (1–4%)	Zero	Unweighted base	Weighted base
	Row percentages				
Reasons for workforce reductions					
Budget reductions/cash limits	2	7	91	180	115
Subcontracting of work	(12)	(3)	(85)	25	15
Method used to reduce workforce					
Compulsory redundancies	15	13	70	286	190
	Means				
Dismissals per thousand employees					
Private manufacturing	27	21	19	2011	1989
	Row percentages				
Any recruitment in last year					
Yes	9	10	80	1923	1780
No	2	2	95	121	200

Figures in brackets are based upon unweighted base of less than 50 and should be treated with caution.
Row percentages may not total to 100 because of rounding or because some workplaces could not be classified.

However, without any measure of whether workplaces with skill shortages had subsequently met their requirements with short-term contract workers, we cannot infer too much from this association.

With respect to freelancers (including home-workers) the patterns were rather different, largely reflecting their concentration in manufacturing industry. To begin with, as stated earlier, there was no clear association, either positive or negative, with the use of 'traditional' forms of numerical flexibility – part-time working and overtime working (Table 3.6). The use of freelancers was not associated with workforce stability or change in either direction over 1, 3 or 6 years, as recorded in WIRS. Nor was it associated with recent workforce reductions. However, in the few cases where 'subcontracting of work' was cited by managers as a reason for workforce reductions there was a noticeably higher incidence of the use of freelancers. Compulsory redundancies, rather than other methods, were more commonly imposed in workplaces that were high users of freelancers. So were dismissals for non-redundancy reasons. Both of these pieces of evidence accord with the higher incidence of freelancers in smaller scale, labour intensive manufacturing. Recruitment of employees had more often recently been carried out in high users of freelancers.

In terms of managerial flexibility to organise work, there was a positive association between such flexibility and a high use of freelancers. This association was, however, only apparent in manufacturing (where freelancers were more commonly used) and in the public non-trading sector (where they were less common). In both of these sectors the pattern was clearest in relation to lack of trade union opposition to management proposals. In manufacturing the relationship was particularly stark: union constraints were reported in only 1 per cent of 'high' users of freelancers, but in 13 per cent of non-users. It would be difficult to dismiss this association as spurious. To some degree it may be just a reflection of the higher use of freelancers in smaller, non-union workplaces. Part may also reflect union opposition to the employment of subcontractors and freelancers. More generally it seems likely that a high use of freelancers reflects an approach to the management of labour that places emphasis on 'management's right to manage'.

WIRS results for 1984

Almost the whole of the above analysis was repeated using similarly or identically defined variables from the 1984 WIRS. The questions referring to management flexibility regarding work organisation and a few others were new in 1990 and have no 1984 equivalent, but well over 90 per cent of the tabulations produced on the 1990 data could be replicated on the earlier survey results. The broad picture was virtually identical. The distributions of the intensity of use of non-standard workers were very similar. Moreover, the characteristics that distinguished high users of either of the main type of non-standard worker were practically the same in both surveys. It is against the background of this stable patterning in the use of non-standard workers that the following findings should be set.

Short-term contract workers

Our 1984 variable, distinguishing high, low and non-users of short-term contract workers, used the same cut-off (5 per cent of the workforce) as in 1990. On this basis 'high' users increased slightly, from 7 to 10 per cent of workplaces between 1984 and 1990. Almost all of the increase was in the public services sector, where high users moved from 17 to 26 per cent of public service workplaces. All of the public service industries highlighted in Table 3.1 with higher than average use of short-term contract workers increased their use; in other words, more workplaces in these industries were high users in 1990 than in 1984.

In the trading sector there was no discernible change in the use of short-term contract workers. High users were 3 per cent of the trading sector sample in 1984, compared with 4 per cent in 1990. Low users declined from 7 to 5 per cent. Neither change comes near statistical significance for change between two cross-sectional surveys of the size of the WIRS trading sector sample. Within the trading sector, the industries distinguished in Table 3.2 as having more high users in 1990 than the average were industries that had virtually no high users in 1984. To this extent it seems likely that there was some spread of the practice between 1984 and 1990 to workplaces that were not previously high users; however, in other parts of the trading sector the proportion of high users declined. There were two other characteristics of workplaces associated with an increase in high usage: a high labour cost ratio; and the presence of union members but no recognition for collective bargaining. These relationships are suggestive of increased pressure on management to contain costs in labour-intensive industries and the inability of unorganised workers to resist a greater use of insecure employment contracts.

In the sample as a whole, the indicators of traditional forms of flexibility shown in Table 3.5 also showed very similar patterns in 1984 as in 1990. The main indicator for which there appeared to be differential growth was in relation to the recruitment of permanent staff. Among non-recruiters, 17 per cent were high short-term contract users in 1990, compared with 11 per cent in 1984. Workplaces that had recruited permanent staff in the past year only increased their use of short-term contract workers slightly (growing from 7 to 9 per cent of workplaces). It was also the case that workplaces that had used early retirement and voluntary redundancies to reduce their workforce had increased their use of short-term contract workers more than other establishments. These results are strongly suggestive of the use of short-term contract workers as substitutes for permanent employees, particularly in the public sector where the growth in their use was most apparent.

Another indicator of increased use of short-term contract workers comes from the fact that 'high' users slightly increased the proportion of their workforces accounted for by short-term contract workers. The mean proportion rose from 14 per cent in 1984 to 17 per cent in 1990. (Low users averaged 2 and 3 per cent respectively in the two surveys.) However, remembering that WIRS recorded the numbers of short-term contract workers at any time in the last 12 months, this increase could arise simply because of the use of shorter contracts or higher turnover among short-term contract workers in 1990.

Freelancers

The change in the use of freelancers was even more marginal than that of short-term contract workers. The proportion of workplaces classified as 'high' (using the same cut-off for both surveys) was 6 per cent in 1984 compared with 8 per cent in 1990. Low users constituted 9 per cent in both years. There was no change at all in the public services sector, where usage was low. In industry and commerce, some of the more unusual categories of ownership appeared to increase their use of freelancers: foreign firms, trusts and charities, partnerships and self-proprietorships. A few of the industries highlighted in Table 3.4 as high users in 1990 had increased their usage since 1984; but just as many had not done so. Three types of workplace did appear to have increased their usage. These were those with highly labour intensive activities, those with trade union members but no recognition, and workplaces less than 6 years old. These 'younger workplaces' were predominantly in the service sector, mostly branches of larger organisations and with higher than normal proportions of female and part-time employees (Millward, 1994a, pp19–21). Again these characteristics point towards a management response to competitive pressures and moves towards a more flexible workforce in the absence of organised employee resistance.

Within-unit change using the 1984–90 trading sector panel

The panel of 537 cases interviewed in both the 1984 and 1990 Workplace Industrial Relations Surveys constitutes a unique dataset with which to investigate change within enduring workplaces in employee relations practices. This is the only statistical source giving direct evidence on changes in behaviour or practice within workplaces, in contrast to the general picture of the changes provided by comparing cross-sectional sample surveys, such as the WIRS of 1984 and 1990. We focus here on changes in the use of the two types of non-standard labour: short-term contract workers and freelancers. Where there is sufficient change, decomposing the panel changes can give indications of the types of workplace most involved and perhaps give pointers to more recent and future changes.

An overall assessment of the panel as a research resource was reported in Millward (1994b). A few salient points should be borne in mind. First, the panel sample had a very high response rate (87 per cent) and is therefore a highly representative sample of the population. Second, the interview data were subject to special editing procedures to resolve any possible doubts about whether it was precisely the same establishment that was interviewed about in both surveys; doubtful cases were given special 'overcodes' and such cases have been excluded from the analysis reported here. For these two reasons the data used can be regarded as of very high quality. However, the resulting sample is quite small (385 cases) compared with the cross-sectional samples (each over 2,000); therefore changes need to be particularly clear before being treated with confidence as applying to the population. Third, the questions of specific interest here, on short-term contract workers and freelancers, were unchanged between the two surveys. Fourth, the population to which the panel sample refers is establishments in British industry and commerce employing 25 or more employees in both 1984 and 1990. The exclusion of public service sector establishments is a particular disadvantage with respect to short-term contract workers, since the growth in their employment was mostly, if not only, apparent in this sector.

Changes in the use of short-term contract workers

The classification of workplaces into high, low and non-users of short-term contract workers, based upon their incidence in the 1990 overall cross-sectional sample, was repeated in the panel analysis. The very slight increase in the use of short-term contract workers shown by the 1984 and 1990 cross-sectional surveys was more marked in the panel sample, suggesting that compositional effects somewhat offset the changes observable in the panel. Cross-tabulating the same variable in the two waves of the panel showed that the great majority (79 per cent) of workplaces employed similar proportions at the two dates. Most commonly, of course, they employed none in both years. However, of the remaining 21 per cent of cases, those that increased their usage outnumbered those that reduced it by a ratio of two to one (14 per cent to 7 per cent). In the small number of workplaces that made substantial changes (from being non-users to high users, or the reverse), new users outnumbered past users by 4 to 1.

Given the small incidence of the employment of short-term contract workers and the general stability in their use within the panel, it is inappropriate to carry out detailed or extensive analysis of the types of workplace where change was most apparent. The numbers of cases involved are simply too small. A clear preponderance of workplaces with increased use over those with decreased use was apparent in metal goods manufacture, food drink and tobacco manufacture, hotels and catering and in miscellaneous service industries. There were no industries where workplaces with decreased use clearly outnumbered those with increased use.

Single independent establishments (single-site small firms) had a higher than average tendency to have increased their use of short-term contract workers. There was a slight tendency for workplaces where management had derecognised trade unions in the period 1984–1990 to have increased their use of short-term contract workers. And there were almost no workplaces where the use of short-term contract workers had increased among the dwindling number of workplaces with high levels of trade union membership density. Again, these weak relationships are hardly a firm basis for drawing any robust conclusion about managerial motivations or union resistance to the use of short-term contract workers.

Changes in the use of freelancers

As with short-term contract workers, we constructed variables for analysing change in the use of freelancers in the panel dataset ,using identical definitions to those used in the cross-sectional analysis. Cross-tabulating the same variable in the two waves of the panel showed that a clear majority (71 per cent) of workplaces employed similar proportions at the two dates. Most commonly they employed none in both years. Of the remaining 29 per cent of cases, those that increased their usage were roughly equalled in number by those that reduced it (15 per cent and 13 per cent respectively).

Although increases and decreases were roughly balanced in the aggregate, there were naturally differences in the experience of various industries and types of workplace. Within manufacturing, there was a preponderance of falls in use over rises in use in metal and mineral products and in textiles, whilst the opposite was the case in mechanical engineering. In the services sector, construction, retailing and business services had mostly increasing use and wholesale distribution had mostly falling use. No other industries had a preponderance of either rises or falls.

Among different types of establishment in terms of ownership, the panel results echoed the cross-section results in that partnerships and self-proprietorships had a preponderance of increasing users of freelancers. Head offices of multi-establishment enterprises were notably the most volatile type of workplace in terms of their use of freelancers: only 59 per cent of them had stable usage between 1984 and 1990 (compared with 71 per cent for the whole panel sample), and 21 per cent remained high users over the period. The results also suggested, as with short-term contract workers, a weak tendency for workplaces where management had derecognised trade unions to have increased their use of freelancers between 1984 and 1990. Again, such a relationship cannot be used to draw any firm conclusion about managerial motivations or union resistance to the use of freelancers.

Conclusions

The Workplace Industrial Relations Surveys throw some light on the changing use by employers of some of the non-standard employment forms which are the focus of this study. In particular we would highlight the following:

* Most workplaces do not employ any short-term contract workers or freelancers (including homeworkers). Intensive users of these types of worker are confined to a few industrial sectors, where labour costs dominate the employer's cost structure. New workplaces are also high users of freelancers.
* The WIRS results confirm the earlier analysis of ELUS that these two forms of employment occur in different types of workplace. Only 4 per cent of workplaces used any short-term contract workers and any freelancers.
* Short-term contract workers were generally used in workplaces where overtime working was rare; these two forms of 'flexibility' appear to be alternatives rather than complements.
* Both short-term contract workers and freelancers were more commonly used in 1990 than in 1984, but not greatly so. The increase in the use of short-term contract workers was mostly a matter of their more extensive use in the public sector,

where they were already concentrated. But there was also some spread of their use in industry and commerce, notably where there were indications of management on a 'hire and fire' basis.

- Part of the increase in the economy as a whole in the use of both types of 'flexible' labour, but particularly freelancers, may reflect the decline in trade unions' ability to resist their use by employers.

Notes

1   The trading sector, as defined here and in all the WIRS sourcebooks, includes privately owned trusts and charities, some of which may be non-trading.

2   McGregor and Sproull (1991) report that 43 per cent of workplaces in the ELUS sample using temporary workers reported that some of them were union members, compared with 82 per cent for full-time permanent employees.

3   This clearly overstates their relative labour input because they were most unlikely to have all been employed at the time of the interview (when employee numbers were collected). The question on numbers of freelancers covered all those used within the previous 12 months.

4   Only 1 per cent was unclassifiable.

Chapter 4

Case Study Evidence:
Introduction

In the previous two chapters the changing pattern of use of flexible working-time practices has been described. This has given some indication of the factors underlying changes in working time. However, there is much about why and how practices are used which cannot be addressed using these surveys. Greater knowledge of the use of different practices and their rationale is essential for an understanding of the development of flexible practices in employing organisations and in the labour market. Within this study, further understanding of working-time practices was gained through case studies of employing organisations.

The aim of the case study side of the research was to increase our understanding of developments in the use of non-standard working-time practices. The issues to be addressed included:

- the reasons for using various non-standard working practices and for changes in their level of use over time;
- the perceived advantages and disadvantages of the different types of working practices and combinations of their use within the same employing unit;
- the constraints which employers face in exercising greater flexibility in the use of labour;
- likely future trends in the use of non-standard work arrangements.

These issues could not be addressed in isolation, but required exploration of the issues underlying different labour-use patterns, both of working-time practices and skill organisation. Thus the qualitative research also aimed to increase our understanding of labour-use patterns in general.

The case studies complemented the survey analyses by enabling an exploration of the interplay between production demands, work organisation and labour supply. They also enabled employers' views to be taken into consideration. The case studies examined in detail the nature of the organisation's work and how working time was organised, and employers' views on the appropriateness, costs and benefits of different types of working time, the constraints on change and their plans for the future.

The remainder of this chapter gives details about the case studies: their selection, their characteristics and the type of working-time practices in use. Chapter 5 discusses the rationale for the practices in use in the case study organisations. Chapter 6 presents the advantages and disadvantages of different practices as perceived by employers. Chapter 7 describes the changes that case study employers themselves expected in the future and an assessment is made about future developments, based on all the case study evidence.

The case studies: selection and characteristics

Given the low incidence of the non-standard flexible practices shown by the statistical analyses, in order to understand the rationale for choosing specific practices, it was important to include both organisations without unusual practices as well as those with them. However, in order to explore views on practices which were not used, it was important that the interviewees had some familiarity with flexible practices in general. The case studies were selected from six industrial sectors (business services, hotels and catering, health services, clothing manufacture, oil refining and metal fabrication) which either had a high concentration of non-standard working-time practices or had had a high growth in these practices. Concentration on these industries seemed most likely to ensure that respondents discussed practices from a reasonably informed position. Both this selection method and the smallness of the sample mean that the results should not be seen as representative. Instead they identify the type of factors which are influencing employers.

Approaches to labour-use were expected to vary with the size of the employing organisation and with labour market conditions. Therefore case studies were selected across the size range and across both tight and slack labour markets to give a variety of types of case studies within each industry. A further selection criterion was to ensure that the less common non-standard working-time practices (for example, annual hours, zero hours and term-time working) were used by at least some of the case study organisations.

A form of quota sampling was used to identify 24 case studies, with quotas for the range of characteristics discussed above.[1] Potential case studies in the six industries were selected from a business database. A letter, explaining the study and requesting cooperation, was sent to the person in charge of human resourcing policy (who had been identified by a preliminary phone call). A follow-up phone call was made to get brief details of the organisation and its working-time practices and to check whether the respondent was the appropriate interviewee (that is, controlled policy).

The findings are based on interviews with directors and senior managers in the employing organisations. Most interviewees were, in larger organisations, personnel or human resourcing directors, or, in smaller organisations, the general manager or managing director. The case study covered that part of the organisation over which the interviewees controlled policy for work organisation. For most case studies, this was the whole company (or, in the case of health, the whole health trust). However, in some companies policy control was divided across establishments or across occupational groups and, for these, the case studies covered that part of the company over which the interviewee(s) exerted policy control.[2]

Against a background of the working practices used in each organisation, the interviews concentrated on the organisation's approach to work organisation and the role of flexible working-time practices, and on the perceived appropriateness of specific practices.

The unrepresentativeness of the case studies was confirmed by the high level of involvement of many of the organisations in training and human resourcing. For example, nearly all employees in one case study in the hotel and catering sector were working towards an NVQ; the same company had been awarded Investors in People status; the general manager in another case study, an oil company, was extremely well-read within both practical and academic literature on human resourcing and managerial issues; the director in charge of personnel in a metal company was actively involved in the Institute for Personnel and Development, chairing one of its working groups. Thus, across the case study organisations, there was a much higher knowledge and development of human resourcing issues than amongst organisations across the economy. This was not seen as a disadvantage. Whilst representativeness is often desirable, the case study organisations, by the very nature of their unrepresentativeness, probably provided a better indicator of how other employers may develop in the future.

Brief details of each case study are given in Appendix 3. Table 4.1 gives summary information on the case studies.

Table 4.1   The case studies

| number of employees | local unemployment | Industry | | | | | | |
		business services	hotel & catering	oil	clothing	metal manufacture	health services	Total
1–25	high	1			1			2
	low	1						1
26–50	high	1	1					2
	low	1						1
51–100	high		1	1	1			3
	low				1	1		2
101–250	high			1		1		2
	low							0
250–500	high		1	1	1			3
	low		1					1
501+	high						4	4
	low			1		1	1	3
Total		4	4	4	4	3	5	24

high = above national average; low = below national average

The range of working-time practices

The case studies exhibited a wide range of working-time practices (Table 4.2). Not surprisingly, all the case studies employed full-time workers. Most also used some of the more traditional practices: part-time working, shift working, temporary working and subcontracting. Nine-day fortnights and four-and-a-half day weeks were found only in a few of the case studies and few used the newer forms of working-time practices (annualised hours, term-time working, job-sharing, flexitime, jobs with adjustable hours and zero hours).

Table 4.2   Case studies: working-time practices

	number of case studies
Pattern of working	
full-time, fixed hours	24
part-time, fixed hours	20
nine-day fortnights	1
four-and-a-half day weeks	4
weekend working	15
shift work	14
annualised hours	3
term-time jobs	4
job-sharing	5
flexitime	5
Flexibility over the size of the labour force	
overtime	19
temporary: fixed-term contracts	16
temporary: not fixed term	17
agency temps	7
subcontracting	13
jobs with adjustable basic hours	2
zero hours contracts	1
short-time working	3

The existence of a practice in an organisation tells only part of the story about its use: its use may be highly limited. In the case studies, some practices were used to a very limited extent. This applied mainly to the newer types of practices, but in some case studies with part-time working, a very small proportion of people worked part-time. It is helpful therefore to describe the practices which characterised the case studies, particularly as these differed by industry.

- *Oil refining* case studies were characterised by male, full-time employment and shift working; other practices were used to a very limited extent.
- *Health sector* case studies tended to have a whole range of practices, with newer practices used by a small number of people only; the extent of part-time varied greatly across occupations and case studies.
- *Business services* case studies were characterised by permanent employees (either full-time or part-time), supplemented by a range of temporary working practices and subcontracting.
- *Clothing sector* case studies employed a high proportion of female workers; they used full-time and part-time working, mainly supplemented with overtime working and sub-contracting.
- *Hotel and restaurant* case studies mainly used full-time and part-time employees, working shifts and overtime; temporary work in particular occupations was also a characteristic.
- *Metal manufacturer* case studies tended to employ males working full-time, with overtime and, in some case studies, shifts were used. Subcontracting of certain activities was also a feature.

Notes

1 Quotas were not rigid but were defined within a range, for example, three and five case studies in each industry.

2 As the main aim of the case studies was to understand the interplay between production, labour market and organisational factors, and to gather views of the decision makers and implementers, whether each case study encompassed the whole or part of an employing organisation was not an issue: what was important was that interviewees could discuss these issues.

Chapter 5

The Rationale for the Pattern of Working-time Organisation: Case Study Evidence

The rationales for employer practices are often buried in history. Certain practices have taken root over time and continue undisturbed. To a large extent this has applied to working-time practices: historical practices continue to be used with little thought about alternatives, and changes are made only as an ad hoc response to immediate pressure. However, recently, some organisations have been taking a strategic approach to human resourcing, re-examining a wide range of employment practices. This has affected their approach to working time. Therefore, in seeking to understand the rationale for the current patterns of working time, one has to look at two levels: the strategic and the specific. These are discussed in the next two sections, respectively. The following section then looks at the inter-relationship between working-time practices and other practices. Finally, the chapter summarises our findings.

Strategic and non-strategic approaches to working time

Over the last couple of decades, management theory has placed increasing emphasis on the strategic development of human resourcing. This has encouraged an increasing number of organisations to see personnel practices, including working-time practices, as an important business tool, on a par with financial and production measures, affecting the achievement of organisational aims. Working-time practices in such organisations will be influenced by considerations of a wide range of aspects of the organisation. Other organisations continue to see working-time practices in isolation, only considering practices in response to a direct problem. Across the case study organisations both types of approaches were found.

Strategic approaches: the implementation of business theory

Working-time practices in a small number of case studies seemed to be driven by current prescriptive business theory of treating personnel practices as an important tool for implementing organisational aims. These organisations had been exploring and then implementing ideas derived from business theory by examining a wide range of their practices to see how they could be better organised to serve the business. Two examples demonstrated the range of approaches.

- To maintain its competitive position, an oil products company had been trying to reduce costs, whilst maintaining quality. Reductions had been made in stock holdings, which resulted in greater fluctuations in labour demand, and the company had been moving towards a core/periphery model of employment. The company had reduced its permanent employment to a core of production workers, with a low number of supporting functions (routine maintenance, accounts etc). Non-core elements of the business, for example, catering and cleaning, had been subcontracted, as had non-routine maintenance and some accounting work.
- A hotel had been examining all aspects of service needs and how tasks might be organised to meet needs. Emphasis was placed on the quality of service, and the problem was how best to deliver services to customers as required, at the appropriately high standard. Constraints included difficulty recruiting a high standard of staff and the variability of demand. The hotel had been investigating ways to reorganise tasks over traditional job boundaries (that is, multi-skilling), including separating some tasks into new, narrowly defined jobs. In tandem with this, the hotel had been looking at working-time practices amalgamating or splitting tasks into full- or part-time jobs.

Strategic approaches: shocks and pressures

Strategic approaches had been developed in some of the case studies in response to major shocks or pressures. This was particularly apparent in the health service case studies, which had been propelled into developing strategic approaches by the shortage of nurses which became severe in the 1980s, by financial pressures and by changes in the organisation of the health service introducing a competitive element. These had led the case study organisations to examine the scope for reorganising jobs (to cover different skills), for using different combinations of temporary and permanent workers and for new approaches to working time. Within the case studies, the most innovative approaches to working time were found in this sector, including the introduction of term-time working, job-sharing, combinations of part-time and full-time and changes in the use of overtime and in shift working.

Labour market and competitive pressures had combined to force one of the hotel companies to develop a more strategic approach to working time. In response the hotel had been developing multi-skilling, combined with different types of employment contracts.

Non-strategic approaches

Two factors characterised non-strategic approaches: firstly, change was only considered in response to pressures and, secondly, change, when it occurred, was ad hoc. Thus, unlike organisations taking a strategic approach to working-time, the response to pressure was narrowly focused and not ongoing. This did not, of course, mean that the case studies were not strategic in their approaches to other aspects of their organisation.

Many of the organisations with non-strategic approaches had considered changes to working-time practices in the last few years. As these were in response to particular pressures, they are described in the next section. However, a small number had not considered change at all. Some had had no cause to alter their working-time practices, which were believed to work adequately. An historical pattern of working was maintained without thought to alternatives. Other case study organisations had not considered alternatives despite difficulties. For example, a clothing company with highly seasonal fluctuations in demand had had severe recruitment difficulties. To cope with the seasonal fluctuations, it had an annual cycle of extensive overtime for many months followed by temporary short-time working. Its predominantly female workforce were mainly employed full-time. Both the variations in workload and in income were thought to cause discontent amongst employees. Nevertheless, alternative contracts, such as annualised hours, had not been considered.

It appeared that the organisations which had not considered change, along with some of the others with a less strategic approach, lacked knowledge and sophistication in respect of human resourcing.

The rationale for specific practices

Whether an organisation takes a strategic approach or not to working-time, the circumstances confronting the organisation might be expected to condition the practices used. This was investigated in the case studies. Obviously, the historical pattern of working-time organisation will be an important influence, but other factors were found to influence working time, including: the pattern of demand, the nature of the product and production, the pressure on labour costs, the labour market, industrial relations issues and employer and management preferences. These are described below.

The pattern of demand

The case studies exhibited a wide range of product or service demand patterns. At one extreme, an oil refinery had a level of demand that was constant; for other organisations demand varied across the day (for example, in hotel and catering and in the health service), across the week (hotel and catering particularly), across the year (seasonally or otherwise) and across years. The range of variability was large: for some case studies the flow of orders might alter demand by ten per cent, whereas for others seasonality of demand was much greater and included periods when there was practically no work.

Predictability of demand also varied. Some case studies could predict demand for a year ahead. Others knew the level of demand over the next few weeks or months. However, for some, for example the hotel and catering case studies, demand was not known with accuracy from hour to hour.

Although organisations could take measures to smooth demand fluctuations (see below) variability and predictability of demand were important factors conditioning the types of working-time practices in use, leading to variations in the hours of work for permanent employees or the use of temporary workers or subcontracting.

Flexibility around a permanent labour force

Overtime was the first choice for dealing with demand increases among most of the case studies (the exceptions being in some hotel and catering jobs and nursing). This was the simplest option, easily adjusted and not reliant on the hiring of additional, appropriately skilled staff. In managerial and administrative jobs, overtime was usually worked by extending the working day. This was often a form of 'hidden' overtime, described by respondents as 'they work whatever hours are needed to get the job done' (usually applied to managers) or 'they are very flexible, they under-stand the business needs and come in as necessary' (a respondent describing the informal flexitime of administrative staff).

For operatives, there was more variety, in part because often a group of workers, rather than an individual, was required for overtime. Factors influencing the organisation of overtime included the hours of the day normally worked (and whether there was a shift system) and the preferences of employees. As well as extending normal working hours, for day workers additional evening shifts (sometimes starting a few hours after normal finishing time) and weekend shifts, including Saturday mornings only, were worked. Additional night shifts were introduced for night workers. Where four-and-a-half day working was used, the options included overtime through an additional shift worked on Friday afternoon. However, several of the case studies did not take this option because they believed their female employees preferred working on Saturday mornings to working on Friday afternoons.

The cost of overtime varied, both across case studies and within case studies. Examples of standard rate payments, premium rate payments and unpaid overtime were found, with some organisations operating time-off in lieu (sometimes informally) where overtime was unpaid. With the small number of case studies, it is only possible to speculate on the reasons for variations in payments: possibly jobs where fluctuations were intrinsic to the job (for example, hotel and catering) were less likely to be paid; where overtime required a group of workers, rather than individuals, perhaps overtime was more likely to be paid; and historical norms for the occupation or industry was likely to play a role. However, the extent of variation included, for example, a company where overtime worked on an additional Saturday shift attracted bonus payments, but additional evening or Friday afternoon shifts (for the same workers) did not. Only one case study, a clothing manufacturer paid part-time workers overtime premiums; these had been introduced in response to employee discontent (over working long periods with extensive overtime, followed by periods of short-time working) in a very difficult recruitment market.

Limits were placed on overtime either because the organisation believed productivity tended to decline above a certain level or because employees became resistant. Employee thresholds were often seen as lower for women than for men.

When an increase in demand was sustained or particularly great, approaches other than overtime were sought. In many of the case study organisations, the next step was to hire temporary workers. This option was precluded for some skilled jobs, due to the lack of potential recruits. However, use of temporary workers was not confined to low-skilled work, with examples of recruits to skilled jobs being found in slack labour markets with the appropriate industrial concentration (for example, the sewing machinists in Nottingham) or where the organisation itself had previously made redundant workers with the appropriate skill.

In most case studies, the pay and conditions for temporary workers were the same as for permanent workers, although none of the case studies awarded fringe benefits, such as membership of pension schemes. Both indefinite and fixed-term temporary contracts were found. The latter were sometimes used when the organisation could estimate the period of higher demand, although one case study respondent said that fixed-term contracts were used to help prevent employment numbers creeping up unnecessarily: renewal of a contract forced reconsideration of needs.

The approach of using first overtime, then temporary workers, for flexibility in the face of demand fluctuations was not universal:

- *Outworkers* were used by one clothing manufacturer if more than very low levels of overtime were required. Nearly all operatives were women and the respondent said that women did not want to work overtime. (The respondent also considered output declined rapidly with extra hours.) Outworking was a feasible option because of the low capital costs of production and because the company was based in an area with a high proportion of clothing companies, resulting in a large supply of experienced female machinists who would do homeworking. To keep earnings below either the social security earnings limit or the National Insurance contribution rates, the company gave only small amounts of work to each outworker.
- *Subcontracting* was another option, used by two clothing manufacturers, for anything more than minor increases in demand. (Small increases were covered by overtime.) In one of these companies, whole orders were subcontracted, amounting to about one third of total turnover. Subcontracting had been introduced about three years ago in response to changes in retailers' buying patterns (increasing the variability of demand and shortening the period of orders) to avoid adopting a hire and fire pattern with its own employees. This same company worked what may be seen as an unusual form of overtime for production workers, in which employees worked through their holiday period, notably the two-week annual holiday shutdown. About one fifth of employees had done this over the past two years.
- A mixture of *overtime, outworkers and subcontracting* was used by a clothing manufacturer. Outworkers (who were ex-employees) and subcontracting were used when the further overtime (which was high) was resisted by employees. Some orders were subcontracted abroad.

A different response was found to demand increases where the nature of the additional work was significantly different from the norm and requiring different skills. Examples of these types of increases were found in two case studies, both involving the provision of specialist training by training organisations. In both cases, because such increases were always treated as temporary and because different skills were required, either the work was subcontracted to a self-employed trainer or trainers were recruited on a fixed-term basis.

As well as coping with increases in demand, some organisations needed to adjust to temporary decreases in demand. Obviously, whether any responses were made depended on the size and expected duration of the decline and the emphasis the organisation placed on keeping costs to a minimum. A number of approaches were found within the case studies who did take action in the face of a decline.

- One company, an oil company, redeployed its employees on to general maintenance activities (for example, painting and decorating the factory).
- A large clothing manufacturer, whilst predominantly using overtime to cope with short-term increases in demand and subcontracting work if this were inadequate, also employed a small group of workers on *contracts which allowed hours to be adjusted downwards* if there were a fall in demand: when demand was low, employees would leave early. As employees were on piecework, with a fall-back time rate, this led to savings in wages.
- *Short-time working* was an approach found in two case study organisations. Major seasonal fluctuations in demand resulted in a clothing manufacturer introducing short-time for a couple of months every year. This pattern was unpopular with employees and its unpopularity was exacerbated by long periods of extensive overtime in periods of high demand. In order to avoid statutory payments, the working day was reduced, rather than employees being stood down for days at a time. Another company, a metal manufacturer, used short-time working to reduce costs when demand was low for a sustained period. However, the company was always reluctant to introduce short-time working because it was inefficient (proportionately increasing start-up and stopping costs) and because it caused industrial relations problems. Moreover, the respondent commented that people worked more slowly in order to spread out the work.

In summary, temporary increases in demand in the case studies were addressed by the use of one or more of overtime, temporary workers, outworkers and subcontracting. Case studies which reacted to temporary reductions coped by redeploying employees on to other tasks, used contracts with built-in ability to reduce hours or placed workers on short-time. The choice between the approaches seemed conditioned by historical usage, employers' views on the acceptable level of overtime, the availability of production capacity and the availability of appropriate labour for temporary work or outworking.

Permanent growth in demand

A permanent growth in demand was a special case of fluctuating demand. Where growth was believed to be permanent, case study organisations expanded employment on the existing basis. However, the permanence of a growth in demand usually emerged over time and case study organisations tended to be reluctant to take on permanent employees until they were confident that growth was permanent. Their reluctance was both due to the costs of recruitment and to the disruption to the workforce if, due to higher demand not being sustained, redundancies were necessary. Therefore, the approaches used to cope with a permanent increase in demand would, at first, usually be those described above.

Where the initial approach included hiring temporary workers, these workers might move into the permanent workforce as demand became more certain. However, capital constraints or preferences for daytime working might result in new shift patterns. For example, a metal manufacturer, having expanded output first through the use of overtime working, then through the recruitment of temporary workers (who became permanent), then felt confident enough about the continuation of the higher level of demand to introduce a weekend shift and to recruit specially to this shift. This eliminated the need for weekend overtime which was unpopular with employees. This approach was probably only open to the company because it was operating in a slack labour market where people were willing to work weekends rather than be unemployed, and it could easily recruit from previously redundant employees. Although weekend work was paid at a higher rate, it made better use of the available capital. On other sites, the company had coped with permanently increased demand by introducing a night shift in the same way. However, compared with overtime working, new shifts were costly to introduce (incurring high recruitment costs) and costly if demand fell (short-time working and redundancies) and so this approach was only taken when the company was confident about the sustainability of the demand.

Whilst this section has looked at fluctuations in the demand for labour due to fluctuations in demand for the product or service, a similar issue was raised by one oil products case study in relation to productivity improvements. This company had been improving productivity and expected further improvements, thus their labour demand would fall in the future. Until improvements had been made it relied on overtime to meet demand. Whilst overtime was excessive (and there was concern that employees might rebel, necessitating recruitment), the company was reluctant to recruit as this would make redundancies likely with productivity improvements.

The effects of demand fluctuations on the nature of the main labour force

Whilst the demand fluctuations described above influence the way that additions or reductions could be made to the output of a core of permanent workers, demand fluctuations influenced the working-time practices of the main labour force.

- A business services company, supplying consultancy, had moved from employing a permanent staff of about 60 (of whom 50 were full-time) to a 'core-periphery' model, with ten permanent staff and a pool of about 30 freelancers. This approach was tailored around the highly unpredictable nature of demand experienced by the organisation, although it had been introduced in response to a rapid decline in demand for their services. The intention was to reduce fixed costs and hence risk. The same company had moved their (two remaining) part-timers on to zero hours contracts, on which they worked one to five days per week, depending on demand. The move, although prompted by the decline in business, was also in recognition of the unpredictability of demand and in order to reduce fixed costs and hence risk.

- *Temporary workers* (in preference to permanent workers) were the first choice for staffing banqueting in some of the hotels and for kitchen portering in the restaurant. This approach was used for banqueting because of the high variability of demand, with the number of events and their size fluctuating widely. As was traditional in the industry, each of the hotels had developed a pool of staff who would work as required. In the restaurant, which had also developed a pool of workers, casuals appeared to be used in order to match labour closely to work demand, thus minimising costs, when labour supply (for an unskilled job) was abundant.

The effects of demand fluctuations on the timing of working hours

Variability of demand could also affect the timing of hours of work. In some cases employees worked, informally, outside their normal contractual hours; in one case study the approach to ensuring that an adequate response could be made to demand fluctuations affected the shift pattern.

For professional workers with nominally fixed hours of work, examples were found of demand falling outside these hours and employees being expected to vary their hours, usually within narrow limits. For example, whilst contractual hours in a training organisation were 9 to 5.30, professional staff were expected to alter their hours to undertake tasks which could not be undertaken during these hours. Chemists in an oil products company organised their working time to suit the flow of work: samples for analysis arrived between 7.00 am and 5.00 pm and, sometimes up to 10.00 pm. The chemists themselves organised their working hours to ensure coverage. A similar practice had grown up in the head office of another oil products company, which was resistant to flexibility over working hours, seeing work outside their standard hours (9.00 to 5.00) as incurring additional security, heating and lighting costs. However, a department having substantial contact with external organisations working different hours had been permitted to arrange working time to suit their work.

The ability to respond to temporary increases in demand conditioned the way that a metal manufacturer organised its shifts. Despite high capital costs, it operated a two, rather than three, shift system, allowing overtime to be worked during the week when required. However, at times demand was so high that overtime expanded into Saturday mornings (which was unpopular with employees) and, as a last resort, night shift workers worked a fifth night in addition to their normal four nights. For this company a permanent increase in demand would be serviced by an expansion of capital and maintenance of their existing working-time practices.

The nature of the product and production
Other than demand fluctuations, many aspects of the nature of the work may influence working-time organisation. These may be grouped under the nature of the product, the scale and nature of production and other activities and are discussed in turn below.

The nature of the product
Services and products vary in the need for their availability over the day, in their ability to be stored or shifted over time. These have major effects on working-time organisation. Whilst some of these aspects are obvious, a discussion of the rationale for different working-time patterns would be incomplete without their mention.

Products or services which need to be available over a substantial proportion of the day and must be produced at the time of delivery (that is, cannot be stored) require shift systems. Within the case studies, much hotel, restaurant and some health service work fell into this category. The details of the shifts varied, with people organised on rotating, 24 hour, seven-day week shifts in some of the hotels and health organisations, but with others employed to work solely days or nights or solely weekdays or weekends. Many of these case studies used a mixture of approaches. The choice between approaches was affected by the labour market, concerns over flexibility of staffing, quality issues and cost considerations, as well as the historical pattern of work organisation.

- *Labour market* considerations tended to encourage the use of straight shifts, the separation of night and day shifts, and of weekday and weekend working thus making recruitment easier and improving retention. Weekend working was especially attractive when skill and quality considerations meant that students could be employed.

- Concern over *flexibility* in the allocation of staff encouraged the use of rotating shifts. A hotel, which mainly used 24 hour, seven-day rotating shifts, felt this approach gave greatest flexibility over allocating staff to customer demand. The restaurant used a combination of straight and rotating shifts for waiting staff: the rotating element was to increase flexibility, the straight element was to ease recruitment and improve retention in a difficult labour market. Several of the hospitals also gave this aspect of flexibility as a reason for using rotating shifts.
- The impact of different shift systems on the *quality* of service was another consideration. For example, a hotel had been increasingly employing core staff for weekday only working and recruiting specialist weekend workers, often students. The hotel was primarily a conference and business hotel, so the quality of service during the week was most important. The hotel operated in a difficult labour market and weekday workers tended to dislike working weekends. Providing weekday only shifts increased its ability to recruit and retain quality staff and provide a higher quality service during its important business period. The impact of operating separate night and day shifts in nursing was a concern of all the health service case studies. Traditionally, most employees worked either nights or days. Night and day work differed, leading to different cultures which affected patient service. Night nurses also tended to miss out on training. Therefore all of the hospital case studies had been introducing rotating shifts.
- *Cost pressures* encouraged the use of practices which closely tailored staffing to the pattern of demand. Most of the case studies in hotel and catering placed a strong emphasis on tailoring staffing to demand and, because of the variability in demand within the day for different jobs (as well as demand varying from day to day), these case studies had a multiplicity of shift patterns. For example, even a restaurant employing 25 people had five different shift patterns: office staff worked the same hours each day; other staff were either employed full-time and worked shifts (split or straight, rotating or not or a

combination) or part-time and tended to work fixed hours. However, similar patterns of demand were translated into different working-time patterns across the case studies and these choices seemed to be affected more by managerial views on human resourcing than external pressures (see below).

A small number of case studies were influenced by the hours and days of work of their main customers. For example, a metal manufacturer and a business services company both supplied manufacturing industry. Their major customers worked four-and-a-half day weeks and this encouraged these two companies to change to the same pattern of working.

A second aspect of the nature of the product concerned product or service quality. This has already been mentioned as affecting the choice of shift patterns. In the clothing case studies, it also affected the choice between in-house production and the use of outworkers or subcontracting. One clothing company used outworking for both packing and machining, but was happier putting out packing work, the quality of which could be more easily checked. Another clothing manufacturer, avoided homeworking and only subcontracted complete orders because it was simpler to monitor quality. A third clothing manufacturer, making a more complex and higher quality product, did not use outworkers for machining because of the difficulty of ensuring quality. Again, whole orders were subcontracted to other companies. However, outworkers were occasionally used for packing.

Scale

The scale of demand affected whether jobs were offered full- or part-time. Jobs were offered part-time when the tasks which were seen as forming a job package would occupy a person less than full-time. This occurred in a number of circumstances:

- when the total demand was too low for a full job; for example, a training consultant worked part-time because the total work of the organisation did not merit a whole employee in this area; a secretary worked part-time because the tasks involved working in an isolated area of the plant, from where other tasks could not easily be combined to form a full-time job;

- when the scale of demand did not fit a whole number of people; for example, a part-time accounts person was employed alongside full-time colleagues because the total work required was not equal to that done by a multiple of full-timers.

Conversely, jobs were offered full-time when the set of tasks would occupy an employee for a whole day, five days per week. Some tasks, by their nature, rather than their quantity, were seen as essentially full-time. For example, in a training organisation a trainee required 30 hours' training (and trainers then had marking time) and so the organisation saw full-time employment as essential (although this leaves open the possibility of job-sharing).

However, the tasks which were packaged together to form a job varied across organisations and over time. Factors which influenced this were historical (to the organisation or occupation), but other factors were identified, such as preference (either amongst employees or managers) for full-time jobs or wider business motives. For example, a hotel had re-grouped tasks across jobs. Two years previously the hotel had moved the stocking and checking of minibars from restaurant workers (who had other tasks) to an entirely self-contained job. Restaurant workers tended to forget to check the minibars until after customers had left, reducing the hotel's income. The move to a separate job resulted in the creation of part-time jobs, mainly working 7.00 to 11.00 am. Employment numbers and wage costs rose. However, these were more than compensated for by the increase in minibar takings.

In some circumstances scale affected whether a set of tasks were sourced by permanent employees or not. In particular, nearly all case studies reported using temporary contracts or sub-contracting for special, one-off projects. Examples included building work, special maintenance, consultancy and specialist professional work. The rationale was to gain specialist skills (and, sometimes, equipment) for short-term tasks which, due to their specialist nature, could not result in continuous employment.

The nature of production

The nature of production, both the capital/labour ratio and the way that production was organised, were important influences on the pattern of working time.

Where the capital/labour ratio is high, there is more pressure to ensure that capital is fully utilised, both for extended periods of the day and by ensuring staffing levels are adequate at all times. The more highly capital intensive manufacturing companies (those in oil products and metal fabrication) tended to use more than one shift per day, whilst the less capital intensive clothing companies did not. An example of capital utilisation considerations was found in a hospital, which had introduced shift working for some technical staff in order to improve utilisation of capital. An oil products company, which used continuous production methods and had very stable demand, operated a tight rota to ensure cover. The rota, which fell into 12-week periods, entailed seven nine-day working cycles (mornings, evenings and nights, together with two days off) followed by three weeks continuous holiday. The system allowed little individual control over shifts worked.

Capital considerations also influenced the use of outworking, which was only seen as possible where little capital equipment was required. A clothing manufacturer used outworking for simple machining and packing. Outworkers had their own sewing machines, although occasionally it was necessary to put work out which required specialist machines, which would then be loaned.

The ways in which work was organised also seemed to influence working-time practices.

- Work divided up on Taylorist lines tended to encourage employers to seek full-time workers. However, in some cases this was mitigated by labour market pressures, leading to the employment of part-timers as well. In at least one case, this had led to a reappraisal of part-timers and management were happy to continue employing part-timers even if the reasons for so doing disappeared. It seemed possible that the real reasons for preferring full-timers were not in fact those of the production method.

- Where production required a team of workers (whether formally a team or not) overtime was often organised on a shift basis. Thus, for example, at periods of increased demand, existing employees worked additional evening or weekend shifts, rather than extending their normal working hours by a variable amount of extra time.
- Independence in the conduct of tasks permitted employees to exercise greater control over their working time and sometimes resulted in the use of flexitime. Few of the case studies had formal flexitime systems and all of these were for white collar employees. Whilst the nature of the work enabled the use of flexitime, it appeared only to have been introduced where labour market pressures or employee demand encouraged it. An oil products company whose office workers had flexitime, said it was particularly suited to married women and did not affect their business, particularly as their employees were responsive to business needs. An unusual practice in one of the metal manufacturers gave blue-collar production workers some individual control over their times of work. Until a few years ago, all operatives had started at 8.00, except when overtime was being worked, when employees started earlier. After an extended period with overtime, employees had pressed for optional earlier starts at all times. It had been agreed that employees could elect their start time (out of three choices); at the time of interview, five per cent started at 6.00 am, 70 per cent at 7.00 am and the rest at 8.00 am. The staggered starting time was only possible because of the lack of interdependence between operatives. This form of employee choice over the timing of the hours of work for operatives was only found in one other case study, a hotel company, where part-time room attendants could choose their start time to work within standard full-time hours.

Non-core activities

Activities which were not seen as essential and peculiar to the aims of the organisations, 'non-core activities', were treated differently from other activities and were subcontracted in many of the case studies.

- *Cleaning* was subcontracted in many of the case study organisations. The reasons for subcontracting varied: some said it was less trouble (despite frequently changing cleaning companies due to inadequate service).
- *Non-routine maintenance* was sub-contracted by many of the case study companies and, in some of the smaller organisations, routine maintenance was sub-contracted.
- *Other activities:* a metal manufacturer, which had sub-contracted all non-core business (including transport, cleaning and catering) found it cheaper, saving in management time, and felt it probably provided a better service. This respondent said 'we make cable, we're not a transport specialist'. Similar sentiments were echoed by other case studies. Subcontracting in other case studies was less comprehensive, although of similar activities, for example, a clothing manufacturer subcontracted printing.

The importance of the task to product or service quality appeared to influence organisations over the activities to subcontract. Where a task was seen not to affect product or service quality directly, it might be subcontracted because the loss of control through subcontracting carried little risk for the organisation. However, judgements about the importance of an activity to the business varied: for example, some hotels (four or five star) had subcontracted cleaning, whereas others regarded cleanliness too important to subcontract. One hotel company had ceased subcontracting cleaning, because of the poor standards they had found with subcontractors.

Costs and competition

The need to reduce costs was strong for most of the case studies. For many of the private sector organisations, this was due to competitive pressures and the price sensitivity of buyers. The health sector experienced somewhat different pressures, but the effect was similar: strong pressure to reduce costs and to increase the effective use of staff. Cost pressures led to the use of working-time practices which matched labour inputs to demand and affected the choice between differently priced approaches.

Approaches to *tailoring staffing to demand needs* have been described above. The extent of match was affected by the strength of cost pressure, the capital/labour cost ratio, the labour market and the extent to which the company treated human resourcing strategically. Less strategic organisations, in loose labour markets, were more inclined to use temporary workers. Where labour market conditions precluded this, they turned to overtime or subcontracting.

Those with a more strategic approach, irrespective of the labour market, tended to develop more sophisticated ways to tailor permanent staff to demand. Some developed more extensive core/periphery types of staffing to reduce costs. For example, a business service company used a high proportion of freelancers (up to 30, six of whom were working at the time of interview, with only ten permanent staff), who were on an annual retainer, in order to reduce fixed costs in a business where demand was lumpy. The unusual feature of the annual retainer helped secure their services when needed and also prevented them competing for the same business. The hotels were exploring a variety of shift patterns, combined with multi-skilling. Some hospitals had increased effective use of staff by replacing standard hours working with shifts, to extend the period of use of capital equipment.

Whilst these approaches were aimed at reducing excess labour supply at times of slacker demand, the degree to which this was done could affect the demands on permanent staff. For example, staffing levels in a number of organisations seemed to be geared to permanent staff working at full capacity without adequate allowance for absence. Some organisations were beginning to consider that they had reduced staffing to levels which were untenable over the long term. One company, with a high capital/labour cost ratio, used a core/periphery approach for many staff. However, it treated its production operators as core and would carry them in slack periods despite easy recruitment and a short training period.

Cost pressures also affected the choice between differently priced approaches.

• Direct costs were a consideration for many of the case studies in the choice between, on the one hand, agency staff and, on the other hand, directly recruited temporary workers and casuals. Where possible, the directly recruited staff were used because of the higher direct cost of agency staff. Organisations with a repeated need for temporary workers (such as banqueting staff in hotels and nurses in hospitals) often established a pool system.

- Cost considerations affected the choice between:
  - using overtime and employing casuals
  - using casuals and permanent staff
  - part-timers working longer hours and full-timers doing overtime
  - using homeworkers and permanent employees on site.

For example, a hospital had greatly reduced its use of overtime for nursing staff, relying instead on their own nursing 'bank' (in effect a pool of casual workers, consisting of nurses wanting casual work and their own employees who wanted to work extra hours). This reduced the hourly rate for extra hours. A hotel used casuals rather than permanent staff over bank holiday periods when permanent staff received double time. A metal manufacturer subcontracted work to homeworkers, who received a lower rate than factory workers and incurred no overheads for the company. The nature of the work subcontracted was limited to simple production tasks for which quality control was easy.

Cost, in terms of pay and benefits, did not affect the choice between full-time and part-time employees; pay and benefits were the same. However, some employers saw part-timers as more costly due to additional administrative and management time incurred. Such companies only employed part-timers where other considerations were strong.

Some case studies also mentioned the importance of keeping working-time practices simple. Simplicity seemed even more important to smaller organisations, especially without a specialist personnel function.

One further example of the role of costs (and in this case the measurement of costs) was found in an oil company. The company was under strong pressure from its parent to reduce headcount. Two of the ways it had done this affected its working-time practices. For a group of supervisors, it had moved from 24-hour to shorter coverage which had reduced its flexibility to cover in other parts of the plant. The change resulted in a minor cost saving and it was commented that 'saving four jobs looked good to top management and... [the parent company]'. It had also proportionately increased its use of fixed-term contract workers because they did not count in the returns to the parent company. New operatives were recruited on two-year temporary contracts, in anticipation of an employee retiring (most turnover was due to retirement). The change was cosmetic with, in effect, recruits spending a period on fixed-term contracts before moving on to permanent contracts.

The labour market

Although at the time of the study few of the case study organisations seemed to be affected by general labour shortages, some had had problems in the recent past (particularly in the health care and hotel sectors) and some were experiencing difficulties for certain occupations. The availability of suitably skilled workers in the labour market was a strong influence on working-time practices, either limiting the range of practices which could be used or leading to the development of new practices to overcome shortages.

The use of temporary workers and homeworking was only feasible when suitably skilled labour was available. This occurred mainly when the job required few skills, the local labour market was dominated by the relevant industry, or when previous redundancies had led to a pool of available ex-employees. Shortages of suitably skilled workers in the labour market restricted responses to short-term increases in demand. In these circumstances greater emphasis was placed on the use of overtime. Some companies resorted to subcontracting work to other companies, even abroad. Some of the case studies (in the health sector and in clothing) had got round the problem of the availability of temporary workers by developing a pool of 'regular' temporary workers. This approach was only found in relation to female workers and seemed to rely on using women seeking occasional work whilst bringing up children, or who had substantially withdrawn from the labour market towards retirement.

Labour shortages had also altered the working-time practices of permanent employees. This was particularly marked in the health sector, where a long-running, extreme shortage of nurses had led to employers introducing a multitude of working-time practices to encourage women with care responsibilities to stay in or return to nursing, including part-time employment (from minimal hours to full-time), term-time employment, job-sharing. Examples of changes in response to shortages were also found in the hotel and the clothing sectors (in response to shortages of machinists). Part-time employment had been introduced in selective jobs to counter labour shortages.

- A hotel, for example, had started to offer room attendant jobs part-time as well as full-time. The number and standard of applicants had risen and turnover fallen. All recruits had been either women close to retirement or women with childcare responsibilities. On recruitment employees chose between full-time and half-time employment, and if part-time, elected their hours of work within the standard full-time day. All part-timers had chosen to work mornings, which had resulted in an unforeseen bonus for the hotel, which could make rooms available to customers much earlier in the day.
- One hotel case study employed over one third of its permanent staff part-time on varying hours. This appeared to be in order to tap into the local labour market, particularly to access catering students, including students on placement.
- Desperation over shortages of machinists had led to one clothing manufacturer to allow an employee to work term-time, despite some of the peaks in demand falling in the school holidays.

Employers' treatment of part-timers (and others on less than full-time contracts) varied. Very few of the case studies employed part-timers on less than sixteen hours and none thought they employed anyone for less than eight hours per week. Terms and conditions tended to be identical for part-timers and full-timers, although one clothing company which did not like using part-timers, would only offer them short-term contracts to indicate that full-timers were preferred, and to ease the laying-off of part-timers before full-timers when demand fell. This contrasted greatly with the health sector organisations which tried to emphasise that all employees, irrespective of their hours of work, were equally valued and treated. Both equal and unequal regard for part-timers was found elsewhere in the clothing and the hotels sectors. Part-timers rarely received overtime payments until they worked above standard full-time hours, although one clothing manufacturer did enhance pay for part-timers working above their contractual hours.

Shortages could also affect shift patterns. Some of the hotels and a metal manufacturer employed people on a night shift only basis. Some hotels and another metal manufacturer employed people on weekend shifts only. These types of patterns existed because it was easier to recruit separately to weekend work and weekday work and separately to day shifts and night shifts.

Changes in working time in response to shortages were only found for 'women's jobs' or where a student market could be tapped; for adult men, improved pay seemed to be the usual tool for reducing shortages.

Employee preferences

Employees' preferences affected employers' responses to shortages, as described above. However, they also affected working-time in other circumstances. In some cases this was part of a general policy; in other cases it was ad hoc, in response to individual requests.

A willingness to operate working-time practices which accommodated employees' preferences was a result of a commitment to equal opportunities in some organisations. One, a training company, allowed employees to move between full- and part-time working in some jobs. The health sector case studies allowed movement between part-time working, term-time working and jobsharing. All of these examples were of organisations where part-time employment was considered by those in charge of human resourcing as in no way inferior to full-time, whilst part-time employees were believed by management to be no less dedicated to the job than full-time employees. The main restriction on choice was in the few cases where the job itself was believed to require more than part-time attendance. For example, trainees in the training company received 30 hours training per week and this was delivered by the same trainer, who also had preparation and marking commitments. The company therefore believed that the trainers had to be full-time. The possibility of more than one person delivering the training per trainee was not considered.

Where equal opportunities were not a consideration, there was usually some other pressure leading to changes which employee preferences conveniently matched. For example, a consultancy with highly variable demand, which had suffered a dramatic fall in demand, had moved from a permanent workforce to a largely freelance workforce and to zero-hours contracts to reduce costs. This was also seen by the company as responding to employees' preferences, with a highly paid, professional workforce who sought greater control over their working life, including the ability to trade pay for leisure. However, it seems more likely in this case that employee preferences (or choices) assisted the company to alter practices, which would not have been altered solely because of those preferences.

Beliefs about employee preferences also affected the pattern of overtime. Some employers felt women and men had different preferences. In some case studies, where occupations were sex segregated, the 'female occupations' did not do overtime, because it was expected that they did not wish to. In others, overtime was worked on Friday afternoons, which was believed to be disliked by women and so women were not expected to work overtime. In a clothing company, employing almost only women, overtime was mainly worked on Saturday mornings for this same reason.

It was not uncommon to find a small number of staff with different working-time contracts to the norm in the company, where an ad hoc response to individual preference, rather than policy, had created the difference. Examples included staff working part-time or jobsharing and a degree of flexibility being operated over starting and finishing times. The latter was found not only for office staff but also for production staff in a metal manufacturer, where production staff were allowed to choose one of three start times. Other examples included:

- A clothing manufacturer employing almost 70 people employed two pensioners on the same job, half time each. This had been instigated at the individuals' request, but worked well for the company as both would work full-time at busy periods and, due to being over retirement age, both could be laid off during slack periods without incurring any statutory payments.

- An oil products company employed a very small proportion of staff part-time or on a job-share basis at head office. This had grown over the last ten years, with the impetus coming from female employees who wished to move to part-time work. The (mainly male) management had been resistant and part-time working remains confined to lower level administrative jobs and to women.

Many employers stressed that employee preferences were taken into consideration in drawing up shift rotas, in some cases resulting in some individuals working straight shifts within a rotating shift system. Others, whilst taking some account of individual preferences, deliberately included some rotation for everyone. This was in order to maintain a flexible approach or to ensure employees remained familiar with different work at the different times of day.

Turnover, performance and morale

Beliefs about the effect of certain practices on turnover, performance and morale affected the choice of working-time practices, including the use of temporary workers, the use of part-timers, the extent of overtime and the type of shift system.

Concerns about turnover, performance and morale led some organisations to offer permanent employment wherever possible.

- For example, although temporary contracts were the norm among its competitors, one of the case study training organisations offered permanent contracts to most of their employees because this was seen as a major way to develop high quality performance: permanent contracts resulted in much higher staff commitment to their jobs, as well as lower stress and lower turnover, both also improving quality. A side effect was the high number of job applicants. However, the organisation felt it had to employ some people on fixed-term temporary contracts where the continuation of work was uncertain, including to cover for maternity or sickness.

Performance considerations influenced some of the case studies in their choice of the means of acquiring temporary workers.

- For example, because of the low quality of agency staff, a hotel had moved from agency casuals to develop their own pool of casuals for housekeeping, banqueting and health club staff. This pool of workers were given training, but were not guaranteed any employment.

For some, part-time employees were not believed to offer the same degree of commitment as full-timers and jobs were only offered full-time.

Many of the case studies mentioned a desire to keep total hours of work low and not to use extensive overtime. Some said that productivity declined rapidly when total hours were more than about 45 to 48 hours per week; another saw problems of quality rising with hours. Systematic paid overtime was only reported by one case study company, a metal manufacturer, and the company was working to reduce this.

Similar considerations came into play in relation to split shifts, which were being eradicated within the hotel and catering case studies. Most respondents also had strong moral objections to split shifts, seeing them as unfair on employees.

Fixed-term contracts were used in several organisations for recruits to try to ensure that permanent employment was only offered to those of a suitable quality. For example, a metal manufacturer used short-term contracts as probationary periods for recruits to the higher quality area of production. If employees performed satisfactorily over the period of two three-month contracts they were recruited on indefinite contracts. Pay and conditions were the same as for permanent employees, except that temporary workers were ineligible to join the pension scheme.

Coverage for absence

In earlier sections the matching of labour supply to fluctuations in demand was discussed. In this section, the influence of fluctuations in the supply of employees, that is, absence, on working time is examined. The need to resort to special measures to cover absence will be partly dictated by the size of the organisation: scale considerations make it easier for larger organisations to allow and plan for absence. It will also be affected by the tightness of staffing levels. Where staffing is tight, special measures for covering absence are more likely to be needed. Within the case studies, coverage for absence was handled in a variety of ways.

For *substantial and fairly predictable absence,* such as long-term sickness and maternity leave, temporary fixed-term contracts were used and holidays. However, a large oil products company said that most absence in its head office could be covered by reallocation of tasks amongst permanent employees. Not surprisingly, small organisations would tend to need to cover long-term absence by recruiting on a temporary contract, whereas for larger organisations this was only necessary to cover specialist skills within the organisation or where staffing was very tight.

Temporary fixed-term contracts were also used in some circumstances to cover holiday absence. Two companies used this approach to cover essential specialist skills only. As with the use of temporary workers in other circumstances, the availability of appropriately skilled labour was crucial.

- An oil company needed specialist drivers (of a type who were not available with most employment agencies). Because of its high pay rates and because of the high level of local unemployment (including its own redundant employees), it was able to employ drivers on fixed-term contracts to cover the summer holiday period.
- In another oil company, specialist needs were a factor in employing the same three women, all past retirement age, as cover for holidays of Board members' secretaries. This practice went against the company's normal approach of only providing permanent employment and was likely to cease when the specific individuals gave up working completely.

Another company used temporary fixed-term contracts as holiday cover for low-skilled operator jobs. This small business services company recruited students.

Less predictable and shorter-term absence was partly covered through overtime, agency temps and casuals. However, few of the case studies, outside the health service, reported using agency temps, preferring to use overtime or casuals. An oil products company used agency temps for secretarial and clerical work in its head office when necessary, but it found that quality and productivity were lower, whilst cost was higher. In the health sector, all three approaches (overtime, casuals and agency temps) were used. The balance between them was governed partly by demand (specialists and more senior nurses were sourced using overtime) and partly by costs. In all the health organisations, due to their costs, agency temps were used only when other approaches failed, and some organisations also used overtime as little as possible, whereas others preferred to use a mixture of overtime and casuals. In order to reduce staff costs, one health employer made permanent nurse employees who wanted to work additional hours register with the nursing 'bank' and these nurses worked (and were paid) as 'bank' staff when they did extra shifts. Across the health organisations, 'bank' staff either received the same, or slightly higher, hourly pay as permanent staff (but lower than overtime rates), but their pay did not attract other benefits (such as pensions), nor were they necessarily paid at more than the lowest grade.

Managerial preferences and historical factors

Cutting across these reasons for using different types of working-time practices were managerial beliefs about different practices and about different groups of workers and historical practice.

Sex-stereotyping of practices and occupations was very apparent. Where the job was thought of as a 'male job' the work would be organised on a full-time basis; with the exception of consultants in hospitals, part-time employment was found in female or non-sex stereotyped jobs. However, consultants' part-time contracts, enabling the combination of private or research work with NHS work, tended to be voluntary: this was a major difference from most part-time jobs in other case study organisations.

Similar stereotyping was also found in some companies in respect of shift work. Although women worked shifts in the service sector case studies (in the health and hotel sectors), the manufacturing sector saw shift work for women as difficult and tended to avoid it. In particular, night shifts were ruled out.

Among some employers a strong preference for *full-time employees* was exhibited. This was particularly marked in some of the hotel and catering case studies, where the pattern of demand was difficult to match to full-time jobs. Here, instead of introducing part-time work, some case studies had introduced flexibility within and across departments in order fully to utilise full-time workers. This was particularly necessary when moving away from split shifts. The rationale often seemed to be that part-time was linked with the idea of temporary or casual working and part-time employees were not seen as being as committed to the organisation. A similar preference was apparent in a metal fabricator, where the respondent saw the high cost of machinery as precluding part-time employment. One of the oil products manufacturers, employing about 150 people in addition to operatives, stated its 'marked preference' for full-time workers: it had only two people working part-time.

However, this type of approach had broken down in the health service, which, owing to severe labour market difficulties and the availability of nurses with childcare responsibilities, had introduced extensive part-time employment. The health service case study respondents laid much stress on emphasising to managers and other employees that part-timers were as equal and valuable a part of the workforce as full-timers. A clothing company had changed its views on part-timers, after opening up some jobs to part-timers because of labour shortages. Its experience indicated that part-timers were equally good as full-timers, an experience borne out by a hotel which found sickness and absenteeism fell when it introduced part-time working (alongside full-time) for room attendants.

The *historically different patterns of working hours* between manufacturing and services persisted in several of the case studies, with manufacturing companies reporting earlier start and finish times for day workers than service companies and some manufacturers working four-and-a-half day weeks. Traditionally such patterns allowed Friday afternoons for maintenance and cleaning, but this no longer occurred in the case studies. Neither was the space always available for overtime, as women workers were believed to be resistant to working overtime Friday afternoons. In a few of the case studies, similar differences in the pattern of work were drawn between office workers and operatives, with different hours of work and length of the working day.

Differences over *expectations of flexibility* were also discernible between industries and occupations. Managerial staff were expected to work the number and pattern of hours necessary to get the job done. A similar flexibility, but to a lesser degree, was expected of many office workers in the case studies. In some organisations overtime would be paid and, in others, time off in lieu given. Such flexibility was also common amongst hotel and catering workers, with workers being expected to work overtime (including additional shifts) with little or no notice. Overtime for operatives in manufacturing tended to be more formally organised.

Managerial preferences also came into play in the move from split shifts to straight shifts. Split shifts were seen as undesirable, for ethical as well as labour market reasons, and all the case studies which had operated split shifts had been replacing them, usually with straight shifts or part-time work. However, none had yet eliminated split shifts entirely.

The interrelationship between working-time and other practices

Flexible working-time practices may be used in isolation, both from each other or from other practices which address the same problems. However, in some cases working-time practices are substitutes for other approaches or, particularly in the more strategic organisations, are used in a complementary fashion. The main linkages found were between working-time and approaches to smooth variability of demand and multi-skilling.

Approaches to reduce variability of demand

Although for some of the case studies demand was sufficiently stable to allow them to use full-time employees and overtime only, for many case studies variability (and unpredictability) of demand greatly complicated working-time practices. Non-standard working-time practices were one way of dealing with these problems. Another was to try to smooth demand.

Attempts to smooth demand were used in the hotel and catering sector, where special promotions and price reductions were used to stimulate demand in low periods. For example, one hotel targeted conferences and business customers during the week and private customers, both tourists and locals, at weekends. Others similarly marketed themselves for tourism and private functions in the seasonally low periods for business. Seasonal promotions were also used by the restaurant. Seasonality was a problem for some of the manufacturing companies. One, a clothing manufacturer, had been exploring other markets to provide a smoother profile of demand.

Of course, in some industries, the impact of fluctuations in product demand on labour demand may be mitigated by holding stocks or changing delivery periods. Within the manufacturing case studies, some smoothing of demand through stockholding was practised, but for many the level of stocks held was low and few built stocks to cope with seasonal demand. Indeed, one had been reducing stockholding to reduce capital costs and this approach, placing greater responsibility on labour rather than stocks to adjust to fluctuations, seemed to be the direction in which organisations were going.

Neither stockholding nor changing delivery periods were available to the hotel and catering case studies, but some of the training and consultancy organisations did alter the delivery profile of their services in order to smooth labour demand. Managerial practices might also reduce the impact on labour demand through, in effect, carrying staff over slack periods.

Perhaps a note should be added about a metal manufacturer which had tried to improve business security by developing long-term partnerships with its major customers. The partnership arrangements were that the customer agreed to treat the company as their sole subcontractor for precision machining; in return the company agreed to take whatever work was forthcoming. Paradoxically, this had resulted in greater fluctuations in demand, since they were now obliged to respond to every order from the customer. Hence the company had to maintain the capacity to respond to orders and reacted with sharp fluctuations in overtime working.

Multi-skilling and changes in job content

In some of the case studies, a coherent approach was being taken towards job tasks and working time. The aim was to reduce costs and increase staff utilisation in the face of variations in labour demand within the company. The changes led to staff taking on a variety of tasks, which gave greater flexibility to move staff as demand required. Where demand for a specific skill only occurred at limited times of the day, employers were able to move from part-time employment or split shifts to full-time employment and straight shifts.

This approach had been taken in some of the hotels (although in others, jobs encompassing a bundle of tasks had been split and the jobs moved to a part-time basis). For example, a hotel, had been reassessing all its organisation, including skilling, job content and organisation and working time. They had been looking at service needs and how they might be more cost-effectively supplied, within the quality standards required. Most of the changes were aimed at increasing flexibility over staffing, enabling smaller teams to be able to respond to demand and to cover for absent staff. At the time of the interview, multi-skilling had been introduced for receptionists/telephonists and for room attendants/ linen porters. This did not affect working time, but did affect ability to respond to demand and absences. In the future, room minibar tasks might be moved to housekeeping, thus enabling a task which was concentrated on part-timers working a 7.00 to 11.00 am shift to be taken in to full-time jobs. Similar approaches were being taken to waiting staff, so that they could work across all main meals (in hotels, waiting is commonly split between part-time breakfast staff and full-time staff serving lunch and dinner) and in bars and lounges. This would result in more full-time jobs and fewer part-time. It would also reduce or even eliminate split shifts.

Health organisations had been taking a similar approach for care workers and for some community health workers. For both groups, tasks tended to be lumpy during the day. Care workers were organised into teams to provide all the non-medical care for patients. Job demarcation between workers was eradicated, resulting in employees being presented with tasks across the day. Community health workers in one organisation were being trained to provide a wider range of services so that they could work longer hours.

Multi-skilling was also used by an oil products company so that operators could provide cover for absent colleagues. This enabled the company to operate at lower employment levels and to maintain a rigid shift system.

Summary

Each employing organisation is subjected to many of the factors described above and their influence on working-time practices should not be seen as deterministic. Even among 24 case studies, similar pressures led to different responses. Therefore, in this section, the main themes and factors influencing working-time practices are drawn out.

Firstly, some organisations are more strategic than others. They have greater knowledge of different approaches and frequently reconsider different types of approach. Such organisations are more likely to develop working-time practices appropriate to changes in their business and the labour market.

Secondly, fluctuations in demand will govern the degree of numerical flexibility required. A variety of responses are feasible and the choice between them will depend on other factors. The main factors are:

- historical practices (and the level of strategic thinking);
- pressures on labour costs. Pressures may be due to price competitiveness, the capital/labour cost ratio (the lower the ratio, the greater the pressure to reduce labour slack);
- the availability of appropriately skilled labour: this will affect the choice between extending the hours of employees and taking on temporary workers. The training period for employees will play a part in this, but both high or low skills may either be in supply or shortage;
- product or service quality concerns: the greater the emphasis on quality the greater the pressure to use existing employees; similarly the difficulty of checking quality will affect the approach;
- industrial relations issues and morale, particularly with respect to changes potentially resulting in redundancies at a later date, or short-time working;
- employee preferences, which will affect the level of overtime acceptable.

Thirdly, occupational segregation by sex appears to have a major influence on the working-time practices used. This seemed to work in two ways: sexual stereotyping and responding to labour market needs. The view that, if it is a man's job, then it should be full-time (and, generally, permanent) was common. Similarly, shift working was more accepted for men's jobs. Although less common, many of the case study employers saw, for women's jobs, temporary, outworking and part-time employment as acceptable. However, from the case study evidence, it appeared that the employment practices deemed appropriate to the main group of workers in the organisation influenced those offered to other workers. Hence in 'male' industries, women in 'female occupations', for example, administration, seemed less likely to be offered part-time (or similar) employment.

Where serious labour market difficulties had been encountered and where the jobs were 'women's jobs', employers had attempted to respond to women's specific working-time preferences, where these were not for full-time employment. Whilst this approach may make it easier for some women to work and may be less effective for men, it is interesting to note that labour shortage in female occupations may be being tackled without resort to the more traditional approach of competing for employees through raising pay.

Fourthly, working-time practices should not be seen isolated from other practices. The need for specific practices is influenced by the implementation of other approaches, notably practices to reduce variability of demand and to increase the range of job tasks for each employee. Some organisations develop their practices in the light of these linkages, whilst others, despite the interactions, see each practice as separate and change practices in reaction to the most pressing problem.

Chapter 6

Employers' Views on Working-time Practices: Case Study Evidence

The previous chapter has described the rationale for each organisation for the working-time practices they used. Of equal importance in understanding the development of practices are employers' views on the advantages and disadvantages of each practice, whether in use or not. Although these issues were partially addressed in the previous chapter, by concentrating on the rationale for using a particular practice, other advantages and disadvantages of a practice have only been touched on and views on practices not in use have not been given. This chapter, therefore, presents the views of case study organisations on each type of working-time practice and the circumstances under which they might be used.

Working-time practices can be seen to fall into two main types: those that primarily confer the ability to adjust the quantity of work for the organisation (practices affecting flexibility of output), and those which affect when or by whom a set quantity of work is done (practices affecting the pattern of working). These are discussed separately below. The next section examines employers' views of the advantages and disadvantages of practices affecting the pattern of working and the following section focuses on practices which allow variations in the number of hours worked over the whole organisation. The final section discusses the implications of the advantages and disadvantages of the different practices.

Advantages and disadvantages of one practice have to be discussed in relation to another practice. Irrespective of the working practices within the organisation, respondents tended to treat full-time, permanent, day working, with fixed times of working, as the norm against which to measure other practices. Therefore practices are compared with this norm, in most of this chapter.

Practices affecting the pattern of working

A number of practices which affected the pattern of working were examined. They can be seen as falling into three groups:

- practices affecting the number of contractual hours per employee:
  - full-time
  - part-time
  - job-sharing
  - term-time working
- practices determining the range of times of work:
  - day working
  - shift work
  - number of days per week
- practices affecting flexibility over the times of work:
  - fixed hours
  - flexitime
  - annualised hours

Practices affecting the number of contractual hours
Full-time versus part-time

Employers' perceptions of the advantages and disadvantages of part-time work varied greatly across the case studies, even for similar jobs. Before describing the nature of these advantages and disadvantages it is important to understand the background to these differences. Firstly, in the case studies, with a few exceptions, part-time work was seen as relevant only for jobs employing females: women might work part-time but men did not. This meant that part-time employment was not considered for 'male' jobs. The few exceptions to this were in an hotel which employed a substantial number of students; some professional jobs where employees wished to combine employment in more than one post (for example, hospital doctors combining hospital employment with a university research post); and in some health sector organisations which had general policies on working time.

Secondly, perceived advantages and disadvantages of a particular working-time practice are affected not only by objective facts but may also be affected by prejudice. For some of the case studies (notably those in oil and metal manufacturing) with a high proportion of male employees, it was understandable that part-time working was seen as irrelevant to their main workforce. However, these organisations employed women in other occupations and part-time employment might therefore have been worthy of consideration, as it might in organisations with a mixed or female workforce. Despite this, the case studies with a high proportion of male employees seemed to see only disadvantages in part-time working and only used it in exceptional circumstances. This suggests a bias against part-time working.

Among the case studies with predominately female or mixed workforces, views were more mixed. A few employers (some of the business service, hotel and restaurant employers) acknowledged both advantages and disadvantages to part-time working and seemed able to consider the appropriateness in relation to specific circumstances; others (notably in the health service, but also a clothing manufacturer) appeared to have shed their prejudices after labour shortages forced the use of part-timers; whilst the other case studies (in clothing and business services), whether users of part-time working or not, were similar to the oil and metal manufacturing case studies, identifying problems but not advantages and seemed biased against part-time working.

Thus the following advantages tended to be identified by those who had either introduced part-time working on an ad hoc basis in very specific circumstances or were not biased against part-time employment. Disadvantages were identified by all groups. The advantages of part-time employment were seen to be:

- cost: to cover tasks which occurred in certain parts of the day only;
- cost: to source jobs where the quantity of work required substantially fewer hours than a full-time job;

- labour supply: to attract enough female employees to the organisation: due to either shortage or accepted practice;
- labour supply: to attract a better quality of female employee, especially previous employees or women who had worked in the same occupation;
- cost and flexibility: the ability to extend hours without paying premium rates (this tended to be seen as an added bonus, rather than a reason for employing part-timers).

Disadvantages of part-time employment were seen as:

- lack of commitment among part-time workers, resulting in poorer quality of work or higher turnover;
- additional administrative and management costs (payroll administration, managing and training more workers);
- flexibility and control: it was easier to arrange shift times with full-time than part-time workers;
- cost: in professional and administrative jobs where the amount of work was full-time, employing part-timers led to the need to recruit more people and for these to liaise.

Job-sharing

Job-sharing was a type of part-time working and was used where it was believed that a full-time job could not be separated into two, but required liaison between part-time employees. Job-sharing was found in a number of the case studies but, except in the health sector, was on an ad hoc basis and confined to administrative jobs. Several of the health sector case studies had a policy allowing job-sharing in all jobs, unless operational factors precluded job-sharing. In this sector, job-sharing was found not only in administrative jobs, but also in professional and managerial jobs. Apart from in the health sector, job-sharing was only introduced with reluctance and sometimes in the face of hostility among line managers.

Disadvantages, identified by organisations with job-sharing as well as those without were:

- cost: of recruitment, finding two people to work together;
- cost: liaison between the two job-sharers.

Advantages of job-sharing were only identified by case studies in the health sector, where the disadvantages of job-sharing were seen to be outweighed by the following benefits:

- labour supply: ability to recruit or retain good quality workers;
- quality: differences in terms of skills and experience between the job-sharers resulted in the employer getting more than one person;
- dedication: job sharers were thought to put in more hours pro rata than their full-time equivalent and to be more productive within the time worked.

Term-time working

Term-time working is a special form of part-time employment. It was found in a few of the case study organisations, particularly among those in the health sectors. In all cases it had been introduced in response to severe labour shortages and the advantage of this practice was seen as:

- labour supply: ability to recruit or retain good quality workers.

Other case study organisations had not considered term-time working and, with one exception, did not recognise any advantages to its use. However, the non-users saw the following disadvantages:

- employers did not perceive a demand from employees or potential recruits. For example a clothing manufacturer said that their female employees used nurseries, family and friends to look after their children during school holidays;
- the pattern of demand did not suit this pattern of labour supply, for example, peak demand occurred during school holidays.

With one exception, the non-users were not interested in introducing term-time working. The exception, a hotel with difficulties recruiting and retaining good quality staff, thought that term-time working was a practice they should consider.

Practices determining the range of times of work

Shift working

In the case studies, shift working was found in manufacturing, in the health sector, in the hotels and the restaurant. The nature of the shifts were rather different between the two sides of industry.

In the *manufacturing* case studies, with two exceptions, working was confined to weekdays (except where weekend shifts were occasionally used for overtime). Cases were found of day-time shifts only, separate night and day shifts and 24 hour rotating shifts, but each organisation had a small number of shift systems covering all employees who worked shifts. Some clothing case studies only worked shifts when overtime was required. Employees tended to work to a fairly predictable pattern.

In the *service sector* case studies, many jobs continued over weekends and some covered 24 hours per day. Cases were found of day-time only shifts, separate weekend and weekday shifts, separate night and day shifts, and 24 hour-rotating shifts. A range of shift patterns were found within each organisations as well as across organisation, and some even had differing patterns within occupations. Some employees worked fairly predictable patterns, whilst others did not, with shifts fixed a short time in advance in anticipation of demand.

The main advantages of shift work (and the reason for instigating it) were:

- to cover a pattern of demand which extended beyond the normal working day;
- to ensure better utilisation of capital – a particular advantage if the capital/labour ratio were relatively high.

The former advantage was reported by case studies with shift working in the service sector only, whilst the latter was a major advantage reported by those with shift working in manufacturing. However, one health sector case study had introduced shifts in some areas of work in order to improve utilisation of capital.

Most respondents in organisations with shift systems did not see shift working as undesirable for employees or as causing recruitment problems. However, despite the extent of shift working by women in the hotel, restaurant and health sector case studies, the clothing manufacturer case studies who did not use shifts saw the potential for shift working for female employees as limited or precluded. For example, a clothing manufacturer said that, theoretically, only day working and evening shifts were feasible because of its predominantly female workforce, but that even evening shifts were precluded in practice because it was impossible to find supervisors willing to work evenings.

The different types of shift systems were seen as having their own advantages and disadvantages:

- *Split shifts,* in use in hotels and restaurants, were seen as undesirable on social grounds and leading to recruitment and retention problems. All the case study employers which had operated split shifts had been working to eliminate split shifts for these reasons. However, these organisations saw that they were a convenient (and traditional) way of sourcing jobs where demand occurred at two separate times of the day (notably waiting, but also cooking).
- *Rotating shifts,* in use in the hotel and health sectors, were seen by users as a good way to maintain flexibility over staffing, to ensure that 'night' and 'day' cultures did not develop and to ensure that all staff were available for training (which took place during the day). However, nursing staff were reported to prefer to work either days or nights and a similar preference was reported for some jobs in hotels. Moreover, problems over sleeping patterns and stress associated with rotating shifts were acknowledged by the health sector case studies.
- Separate *weekday/weekend shifts* were seen by users to have the advantage of easing recruitment, with more potential recruits willing to work either weekends or weekdays but not both. The disadvantage, reported by users and non-users, was a loss of flexibility over staffing levels, because employees were not transferable between weekdays and weekends and, sometimes, differences in quality of staff (and therefore service) at different times of the week.

Five-day weeks, four-and-a-half-day weeks and nine-day fortnights
Case study organisations operated over a range of days per week: four-and-a-half, five or seven, or nine days per fortnight. Seven-

day working has been discussed under shifts and the other, weekday, patterns will be considered here.

The main considerations in relation to the pattern of weekday working were customers' patterns of work and the pattern of work of similar local employers. For example, a metal manufacturer said that nine-day fortnights were not appropriate because most of their customers worked four-and-a-half-day weeks; whilst a clothing manufacturer was considering moving to four-and-a-half-day weeks because most local factories did so which was creating demand among their own employees for this pattern.

Thus the advantages and disadvantages of different patterns were not intrinsic to the pattern, but were derived either from:

- matching production to customer contact or
- maintaining good employee relations.

No employers with four-and-a-half-day weeks or nine-day fortnights seemed to use the spare half day or day for maintenance or for overtime working and this was not cited as an advantage of these practices. Indeed, several case studies said that overtime was not worked in these periods because employees preferred to keep this time to themselves and do overtime at the weekend.

Practices affecting flexibility over the times of work

Flexitime

Flexitime was not a common practice among the case studies and formal flexitime (with rules on the number and timing of hours and with full recording of hours) was found only in the health sector case studies. A metal manufacturing company had considered flexitime for administrative staff, in order to ease travel difficulties. However, the idea had been dropped in the face of strong resistance from departmental managers and only weak demand from employees; managers saw flexitime as difficult to manage and the recording system as costly. The disadvantages of flexitime, reported by non-users, were seen as:

- employees needed to be working at the same time: this was considered important not only when employees worked together or in other ways were highly dependent on each other, for example, clothing manufacture machinists, but where employees sometimes needed to contact each other;

- flexitime did not suit customers, for example, a metal manufacturer said that its work was determined by customer times and so was not suitable for production workers, although it might be for some administrative staff;
- flexitime was difficult to monitor and manage;
- employees did not have the necessary self-discipline;
- cost: flexitime increased the period the workplace needed to be open, heated and staffed.

None of the case studies reported advantages to their organisation in operating flexitime, with the sole advantages mentioned being:

- making it easier for women employees to combine home and work activities.

However, this should result, if not in easing recruitment, but improving retention and reducing absence, both advantages to the organisation.

Despite objections to a formalised system of flexitime, many of the case studies allowed flexibility in starting and finishing times for some staff. In most cases the extent of variability was limited (perhaps to an hour) and tended to be confined to administrative, managerial and professional staff, as other employees were believed to need to work the same hours. However, some other jobs in these organisations would not have been disrupted by some flexibility, and reluctance to allow employees some control over starting and finishing times may have related to other disadvantages described above.

Two companies did allow manual employees choice over working time, although without the flexibility of flexitime. On recruitment, a hotel allowed part-time room attendants to choose their times of work, whilst a metal manufacturer allowed manual employees a choice of three starting (and therefore finishing) times. The latter had not been considered (and would not have been thought possible) until an extensive period of overtime (worked at the beginning of the day) encouraged employees to exert pressure for earlier start times and the company could see no reason why this could not be accommodated.

Annualised hours

Views on annualised hours seemed to be partly conditioned by lack of knowledge about the practice. For example, one company with a fairly predictable workload over the year, but which fluctuated seasonally, did not see how annualised hours were appropriate. It also considered that employees would be resistant to annualised hours, despite currently encountering problems because of fluctuating between periods with extensive overtime and short-time working. However, where there was greater understanding, views on the practice varied.

For those with some understanding (although not experience) of the practice, the advantages of annualised hours were seen as:

- reducing costs through better matching of permanent employees' work to demand and reducing average cost per hour where demand varied seasonally only;
- reducing costs through better matching of permanent employees' work to demand and reducing average cost per hour where demand varied;
- increasing flexibility over allocation of permanent staff;
- an alternative to using casual staff, with staff on annualised hours less able to refuse work and more loyal.

For the same respondents, the disadvantages and lack of appropriateness of annualised hours to their organisation were seen as:

- their workload lacking the degree of variability necessary for annualised hours;
- demand being cyclical rather than seasonal and therefore annual staff needs could not be estimated;
- the system being too complicated, particularly where labour turnover was high;
- annualised hours shifting some control over hours of work from management to employees and therefore undesirable.

Practices affecting flexibility over size

Three types of practices primarily enabled employers to adjust the quantity of work in the organisation:

- practices adjusting the hours of permanent employees
  - overtime
  - zero hours contracts
  - short-time working
- the employment of people on a temporary basis[11]
- subcontracting work
  - use of consultants and freelancers
  - homeworkers
  - subcontracting to other companies

Practices adjusting the hours of permanent employees

Overtime

Overtime was the most common practice used to increase output. It was operated in all the case studies, although sometimes only informally. Examples were found of overtime being operated informally in managerial, professional and some administrative jobs (employees were expected to work additional hours as necessary) and formally in other administrative jobs and all other jobs. In the case studies, when overtime was operated formally, it was paid and, in all but one of the case studies, paid at a premium rate; when it was operated informally, it was unpaid, but time off in lieu might be given. Except in one case, overtime premiums were only payable to part-timers once their hours exceeded full-time hours.

The advantages of overtime were seen as:

- offering a highly flexible method of temporarily increasing output, with no difficulties over finding appropriately skilled workers;
- offering a relatively cheap method of temporarily increasing output, as no recruitment, training or layoff costs were incurred.

Its restrictions and disadvantages were:

- difficult to control, leading to cost escalation;
- limited size: overtime was seen as being restricted in terms of employee willingness to work overtime. High rates of overtime, particularly over long periods, met with employee

resistance and thresholds of acceptability were lower among women;

- limited size: productivity per hour was thought to decline above certain levels of hours;
- limited size: unlike subcontracting to other organisations, overtime was limited by the organisation's own capital.

Respondents in the case studies which did not use formal overtime felt labour supply constraints prevented its use. (This was raised in relation to female workforces, where women were regarded as unwilling to work overtime.)

In one of the case studies, an oil refinery, employees were obliged to work extra shifts to cover for unanticipated absence but they were not paid an overtime premium. This was believed to minimise absence, as employees disliked working extra shifts and peer group pressure then kept absence at a low level.

Zero hours

Zero hours was an unfamiliar practice to many of the case study respondents and many gave their views on the practice having been introduced to it for the first time in the interview. None of the case studies had introduced genuine zero hours contracts.

The advantages which zero hours were thought to have were:

- costs: reducing costs through matching labour supply to demand;
- cementing the relationship between employees and employer in comparison with casual employment, making it more difficult for workers to turn down work.

However, all the case studies saw disadvantages to zero hours which greatly outweighed potential advantages:

- recruits would be resistant, thus creating or exacerbating recruitment difficulties. For example, the restaurant had considered zero hours, but felt that people would be unwilling to wait on call. Similarly, the system would encourage turnover;
- zero hours would not develop the commitment required of employees;
- the legal aspects of zero hours were too difficult.

More than one case study respondent said that zero hours conflicted with their company's human resourcing philosophy, which was aimed at developing commitment and attachment.

A similar practice to zero hours, but less extreme, had been developed by a clothing company. This organisation had introduced a contract for a small group of employees where hours could be adjusted up or down depending on demand. This was similar to zero hours contracts except that a minimum number of hours were guaranteed. This type of contract might be seen as more desirable by employers and not present the same problems as contracts with a zero minimum number of hours.

Short-time working

Short-time working was only used by employers when demand fell substantially. Its advantage, described by users, was:

- costs: by matching labour supply more closely to demand when demand fell.

However, users felt that disadvantages were substantial and, among the case studies, the practice was used with reluctance:

- it was disruptive, causing industrial relations difficulties;
- cost savings were relatively low per hour, as employees on short-time tended to stretch work out to maximise the number of hours worked.

The employment of people on a temporary basis

Case study employers had a preference for employing people on a permanent basis. Permanent staff were considered to be more reliable, loyal and committed. There also seemed to be a moral preference for offering permanent jobs: if the work was permanent, then the job should also be. However, temporary staff were used by all the case studies and were recruited:

- to cover fluctuations in demand;
- to cover increases which might not be permanent;
- to cover for absence.

Within the case studies, usage seemed to vary across occupations. The circumstances in which temporary workers would be used in manual and administrative jobs were seen as fairly normal occurrences, whereas, apart from in nursing and research posts in the health sector, the circumstances requiring temporary professional employees were exceptional. This was partly due to lower use of non-permanent professionals and partly because professional work was often subcontracted (see below). The feasibility of using temporary workers was constrained if the training period for the job was lengthy and if ready skilled workers were not available.

In most of the case studies temporary workers were brought in to work in the same jobs as permanent employees, although one group of case studies (hotels) staffed one activity (banqueting) with temporary employees only. The advantages of temporary staff were seen to be:

- the use of temporary staff enabled the organisation to minimise fixed costs;
- staffing on a temporary basis avoided the cost of redundancy (and industrial unrest) if an increase in demand proved temporary;
- if higher demand became permanent, temporary workers provided a ready source of permanent employees and enabled employers to recruit permanently those who had proved good workers.

Disadvantages related to

- the quality of staff;
- difficulty recruiting;
- lower commitment among temporary staff.

Because of these disadvantages, most case studies preferred, where possible, to cover increases in demand by using overtime. However, despite similar concerns over quality, some of the health sector case studies preferred to use temporary workers in nursing (or a mixture of temporary and overtime) because:

- the labour costs for certain types of temporary workers were lower than for overtime;
- in stressful jobs (particularly psychiatric nursing) only limited amounts of overtime could be worked without seriously jeopardising the patient or the employee.

Lower costs due to lower pay rates were also cited as an advantage by a hotel in relation to using temporary workers for bank holidays. Otherwise, temporary workers in the other case studies received the same rates of pay as permanent workers and where, as in most cases, permanent workers did not receive other benefits, the direct costs of temporary and permanent workers were the same.

For cost reasons, several of the case studies had reduced the size of their permanent workforce, leading to a higher reliance on temporary staff to cope with fluctuations in demand or absence.

Different forms of temporary work (fixed-term and open-ended), organised in different ways (through an agency, through a regular pool or via the external labour market) were used by the case studies, each with their own advantages and disadvantages.

Fixed-term contracts were used to cover special projects (that is, out of the ordinary work with a finite life) and fairly predictable absence, particularly maternity leave and holiday absence. Most of the examples of temporary employment of professional workers were fixed-term and included medical research staff working on fixed-term funding. The obvious benefit of fixed-term contracts in this case was that employees could be matched to the period of need or funding. In some case studies fixed-term contracts were also used when there was less certainty about the period of need, with the fixed-term element used to ensure the need for the extra staffing was kept under review, thereby reducing the opportunity for inadvertent increases in staffing.

Open-ended temporary contracts were used where continuation of need was less predictable, for example, when the normal work of the organisation had risen potentially permanently. Obviously, this form of contract matched the uncertainty of need, whilst the explicit temporary nature of the job enabled employers to avoid industrial relations difficulties if demand slackened.

Agency temps were used in administrative and clerical jobs and in nursing. Whilst agencies provided an easily accessible supply of staff, many of the case studies used them as a last resort because of their relatively high cost. Indeed, the health service case studies had largely replaced agency nurses by greater use of overtime and by building up their own bank of casual workers. A further disadvantage of agency workers was the loss of control over selection.

The establishment of a *pool of temporary workers* was an approach used for banqueting staff in hotels and for nursing staff in the health sector. The advantages identified by users of this approach were:

- easier access to temporary workers at short notice;
- temporary staff familiar with the organisation;
- cost (compared with agency staff);
- the opportunity to recoup training costs incurred by temporary workers and thus the incentive to train this group.

This approach has been long-established within hotels, but had been growing within the hospital case studies. Indeed in some of the health sector case studies, the practice was being used not only to replace expensive agency staff but to replace overtime working, with permanent employees having reduced opportunities for overtime, having to sign on for temporary work via the 'bank' instead.

Subcontracting

Subcontracting was used in a number of circumstances: to source activities which were outside the sphere of the organisation's usual activities, both on the demand side, such as an order which was out of the ordinary, and on the input side, such as occasional refurbishment or management consultancy; to source subsidiary activities (for example, cleaning or catering in a manufacturing company); and to cope with fluctuations in demand.

The advantages of *subcontracting activities outside the sphere of usual activities* seen by users and non-users, were that it accessed specialist skills and/or equipment and that the cost was only incurred whilst there was the need. Thus subcontracting saved not only labour costs, but, in certain cases, saved on capital costs. There was no real alternative to subcontracting occasional jobs requiring substantial additional capital equipment. However, employing temporary workers was an alternative to subcontracting activities requiring little capital or human capital only, for example, management consultancy, specialist trainers,

of subcontracting rather than temporary
ly governed by the labour market structure,
with services tending to be offered on a subcontract basis. Some
users of subcontracting preferred this approach, seeing the
buying of a particular outcome, through subcontracting, as easier
to manage than buying time to produce an outcome, through
temporary employment.

The advantage of *subcontracting subsidiary activities,*
identified by users, was in terms of cost, either due to reductions
in management input to the activity or through using
subcontractors offering different terms and conditions to an in-
house service. However, cost reductions could not be assumed
and, in the case studies, an example of subcontracting cleaning
which had resulted in increased costs was found. The other
disadvantage, identified by some users and non-users, was a
degree of loss of control. Consequently, subcontracting could
lead to changes in service quality, either for the better or the
worse. The distinction here between main and subsidiary
activities was important in adjudging the suitability of
subcontracting. Subsidiary activities were those which did not
have an immediate or direct effect on outputs, that is, failures in
these activities either did not lead to output not being achieved to
an acceptable quality or allowed adequate time for corrective
action. This form of subcontracting was used to replace
permanent employment with the organisation.

Subcontracting to cope with fluctuations in demand takes a
number of forms: subcontracting batches of work to other firms,
using homeworkers, and using freelancers, with the latter used
for work mainly requiring human capital only, for example,
training. The alternatives to subcontracting included using
overtime and employing temporary workers. Subcontracting was
preferred to these alternatives in a number of circumstances:

- where alternatives would require investment in additional
  capital;
- where overtime had reached unacceptable or unproductive
  levels;
- where unit costs were lower: this was sometimes the case for
  homeworking.

The main disadvantage, identified by users and non-users, was loss of control, particularly over quality. Obviously this was a more serious consideration in subcontracting a main activity than a subsidiary activity and, not surprisingly, seemed to restrict this type of subcontracting in the case studies. A further restriction was on the availability of subcontractors, either with the appropriate skills or the appropriate capital.

The implications of the advantages and disadvantages of different practices

The advantages and disadvantages of different practices perceived by employers meant that:

- a particular pressure or need could often be addressed in more than one way, that is, in deciding on working-time practices employers could exercise choice and preference;
- because the advantages and disadvantages of each practice differ, the appropriateness of a particular working-time practice will change as the pressures on each employer change.

These have two important implications for the development of working-time practices. Firstly, the advantages and disadvantages identified make it clear that certain practices may be more appropriate for a larger number of employers in particular economic circumstances than in other circumstances. The pressures on employers which make particular types of working-time practices appropriate are affected by external cyclical and secular factors, notably, competitive pressures, the buoyancy of the economy and the labour supply. Thus, the future pattern of working-time is likely to be affected by economic developments and it should not be assumed that working-time practices are phenomena with their own independent trajectory.

Secondly, however, because employers have a degree of choice over the form of practices, working-time practices may change not only in response to economic pressures but also to changing preferences. Preferences themselves may be subject to fashion and, as with other fashions, human resourcing seems to have its own fashion cycle: introduced first by 'leading-edge' employers, followed by other employers; then problems with the new in Taylorism, performance pay and flexitime. There is no reason to assume that flexible working-time practices (which have been subject to extensive promotion and have identified disadvantages as well as advantages) will not also be susceptible to this pattern.

Note

1   Agency temps are included within this group because, in their use, agency temps are closer to employees than other subcontractees.

The Future:
Case Study Evidence

An important aim of this study was to help identify future developments in working-time practices. As part of this, case study respondents were asked about the changes to working-time practices which they themselves expected to make. However, as the discussion of strategic and non-strategic approaches in Chapter 5 indicated, many changes in practice will occur in response to unpredicted stimuli. Many employers' expectations will be grounded in the pressures they currently face, which will not provide a good basis even for indicating developments in the next year or two. However, employers' views on different practices, their preferences and rationales for using particular approaches provide strong indications about how practices might develop. Therefore potential developments can be considered in the light of the evidence presented in the preceding three chapters.

Another consideration in trying to identify future developments is the extent to which employers are able to introduce the changes they consider desirable. The extent to which employers felt constrained in making changes to working-time and the nature of those constraints were discussed in the interviews and the findings are presented next. The chapter then describes the changes in working-time respondents expected to see in their own organisations. Finally, the whole of the evidence from the case studies is brought together in a discussion of the future.

Constraints on employers' working-time developments

In Chapters 6 and 7, a number of factors constraining working-time practices were described. These stemmed from the market and were supply constraints: the availability of skills in the labour market, the supply of individuals to work in particular ways and the supply of capital. Institutional and legislative factors also constrain working-time organisation, affecting the desirability or feasibility of a particular practice and the ability of the employer to implement change. These type of constraints are described below.

Unions

About half the case studies recognised trade unions for consultation. These were concentrated in the health sector and in metal manufacturing, although some of the oil products and clothing companies also recognised unions.

The extent to which unions were reported to be a constraint to changing working-time practices seemed to depend on the relationship between unions and management in each organisation. For example, many of the respondents saw their unions in the same light as they saw their whole workforce: both needed winning over if change were to be successful and unions were no more difficult to persuade to accept change than the workforce as a whole. The difficulties were seen as minor and, for example, one health sector case study said that, whilst their unions might be resistant to change, they recognised it had to occur. However, a few of the case studies saw their unions as brakes on change, either slowing down or preventing innovation. Others paid little attention to their unions: for example, one said 'we sort of operate in a feudal culture; the unions are deferential towards us'.

One of the health sector case studies raised national agreements as a particular problem for introducing new forms of working-time practices. The national pay agreements prevented health trusts from considering work practices as a whole package and only allowed them control over certain practices. For working time this meant that changes which might be expected to encompass payment changes could not be implemented as a package.

... practices which can be seen as enabling women to combine home and work responsibilities. One of the health sector case studies encountering these problems emphasised the importance of information and education to overcome fear and prejudice against certain practices.

As well as a constraint, employees could also be the stimulus of change. In some case studies it was adaptation to employee requests alone which had brought about change (for example, the metal fabricator which had allowed production workers some choice over working times). However, in other case studies employee pressure seemed to be effective only where other factors placed strong pressure on the organisation to change anyway.

Information

Many of the case studies seemed poorly informed about practices which were not in use in their organisation. This particularly applied to the newest practices (annualised hours and zero hours). Lack of knowledge about the benefits of particular practices inhibited consideration of changes which might benefit the organisation. Lack of knowledge about the operational details of a practice, particularly if it were complex (for example, annualised hours), seemed to dissuade full consideration of practices which had been identified as appropriate. Thus lack of knowledge constrained the development of the most appropriate working-time practices. It is therefore worthwhile to consider how case studies gained information about human resourcing in general and working-time practices in particular.

The degree to which employers were informed about working time practices varied greatly. At one extreme were respondents who were very well informed; for example, a respondent in an oil products company, who read widely across the business, human resourcing and technical literature (for example, the *Harvard Business Review, Fortune* and the *Financial Times).* He had also participated in a programme (sponsored by the DTI, he thought) which promoted exchange of information on flexible working practices between employers, through visits between companies and seminars. At the other extreme, and mainly amongst the small organisations, respondents seemed to have no more than a lay person's knowledge of working-time practices and participated in no activities which would keep them informed. Other case study respondents were between these extremes and seemed mainly to gain information from human resourcing journals, such as *Personnel Today* and journals published by the Industrial Relations Service.

For some respondents professional organisations or industry networks were important sources of information. One respondent was an active member of the Institute of Personnel Development; another a member of the Hotel Catering Management Association. Industry networks, of human resourcing specialists, were reported in the health sector and in the hotel sector. Respondents found these very useful for identifying novel practices in their industry and for gaining further information from those operating new practices. This type of approach was not open to all, with one of the metal fabricator respondents saying that companies in her industry did not exchange information because of the high level of competition.

Legal constraints

The potential for legislation, including the European Union Working Time Directive, to constrain the development of working-time activities was discussed with the case studies. Many of the case studies saw no legal constraint on the ways they would wish to organise working time. The few constraints that were felt were considered to be mild. These included:

- a hotel said
  employee cont...
  implementation of change

- an oil products company said
  legislation meant that they had to ...
  orders were low. However, the company
  policy favouring security of employment and
  ...unlikely that legislation allowing easier dismissal would
  changed the practice in this company.

The recent change in employment protection legislation affecting
part-timers was mentioned by one respondent, in the health
sector case study. The organisation considered it important that
part-time employees were seen as equally valuable as full-timers.
Because legislation had previously differentiated between those
working under 16 hours and others, the organisation had only
employed part-timers at 16 hours or more. The change meant
that they would now consider contracts of less than 16 hours.
Although not mentioned by the respondent, it was also possible
that the reason for not employing people at lower hours was also
due to union pressure.

Some respondents discussed what the impact of the European
Union working-time directive would have been, if implemented.
Some said it would have required changes to the way that their
working time was organised. For example, a metal fabricator said
it would have caused problems with their night working and that
they would also have to amend their practice of combining shifts.
Others would have welcomed the directive, despite implications
for their own practices, seeing it as presenting a means of
overcoming opposition to a radical review of working-time
practices. For example, a health sector respondent said that it
would have provided the opportunity to implement substantial
change: it would have strengthened their hand against the
unions, in particular, and against managers.

Employers' expectations of future change in their working-time practices

The case study employers were asked about changes they
expected to make to their working-time practices in the next few

years. Not surprisingly, the pattern of potential changes reflected the behaviour and response to pressures described in Chapter 5. Organisations with more strategic approaches were continuing to continue to review needs, consider a wide range of practices including multi-skilling and introduce changes as appropriate. Other organisations were considering changes in practices in response to changes in external pressures. Five considered they were unlikely to make any changes in the next few years. Because of the similarity between future plans and changes already introduced, this section will only briefly list the changes which were expected, except where those were unusual.

Cost pressures, labour shortages and changes in demand were leading case studies to consider making changes. Excluding the whole range of practices under continuous consideration by the strategic organisations, the changes included:

- increases in subcontracting (to reduce costs; or, in the health sector in response to government pressure);
- the introduction of annualised hours (to reduce costs; to meet legal requirements in relation to midwives and maternity care);
- introducing shift working (to cope with higher demand);
- changing shift systems (to reduce the excessive hours of operatives);
- switching permanent jobs to temporary (to cope with uncertain demand);
- increasing use of part-time working (to replace split-shifts; in response to female employee needs);
- decreasing use of part-time work (in tandem with multi-skilling);
- introduction of flexitime (to harmonise working patterns of professional and administrative staff).

Overall, the picture was of some types of practices increasing in some organisations and decreasing in others in response to different pressures. In few of the case studies were new practices being planned; most changes were either in the extent of use of a particular practice, the particular occupations in which the practice was used or in the nature of the practice. However, it was noticeable that several case study organisations were considering introducing annualised hours, which is still a fairly novel practice. Another practice, which was novel in its application to the selected occupations, was a health sector case study considering establishing 'banks' for administrative and clerical staff: these would be similar to nursing 'banks' and would reduce costs by avoiding premium agency rates for temporary staff. It would also result in a permanent group of workers, who would develop knowledge of working in the organisation. A 'bank' was also being considered for doctors (locums) in response to a growing shortage of locums from their existing source.

Future developments in working time

This section considers what we can learn about future developments in working-time practices from the case study evidence. The approach has been to examine in detail the types of practices the case study organisations use, the reasons practices might be used and the factors which drive or constrain change. It should be clear that, whether strategic in their approach or not, there are factors which strongly influence change in working-time practices and which will influence their future development.

The case study organisations are not representative of employers in Britain. Nevertheless, we believe that the findings from the case studies give a good idea of the nature of changes which are likely to occur under differing conditions in the next five to ten years. The types of pressures and constraints which we have identified as affecting working-time practices are likely to be similar across industries and employing organisations, although they may vary in strength. Therefore the behaviour of the case studies should present a good idea of the nature of change across the economy.

The case studies showed a small number of factors driving the changing nature of working-time practices. These are listed below, together with the types of working-time practices which may be introduced in response to these factors.

- *Management preferences:* favouring
  - full-time, permanent employment
  - straight shifts (rather than split)
- *Cost pressures:* leading to the closer matching of staffing with demand and to tighter staffing; this in turn needs new practices to cope with absence and variation in demand, favouring

- multi-skilling (task alteration)
- shift working (especially where variations in demand over the day, or a high capital/labour ratio)
- employer exercised flexibility over hours (annualised hours, zero hours)
- temporary workers, including 'banks'
- subcontracting subsidiary functions
- subcontracting excess core functions
- *Demand fluctuation:* favouring
  - temporary employment
  - subcontracting
  - flexible hours (annualised hours, zero hours)
  - overtime
  - rotating shifts
- *Quality concerns:* favouring
  - multi-skilling
  - permanent employment
- *Labour shortage:* where the shortage could be addressed with female recruits, this favoured
  - job-sharing
  - part-time employment
  - term-time employment
  - flexitime.

Moreover, a number of constraints affected the practices which were used. In particular, employers' beliefs about employee preferences (particularly, men's preference for full-time employment, women's reluctance to work night shifts or overtime) and employers' knowledge about the newer practices affected the practices used.

These pressures driving change and constraints are important in understanding recent changes which have occurred in working time. In understanding the future, expectations about how the balance of these pressures may change is also of importance.

- As discussed in the previous chapter, management preferences may be influenced by fashion and thus are susceptible to change.
- Cost pressures are affected by both cyclical and secular developments. Whilst secular increases in global competition might be expected to maintain pressure to minimise costs,

emergence from recession may somewhat reduce pressures. In the public sector, there has been strong pressure to minimise costs: changes in such policy could affect the extent to which cost-minimising working-time practices are used.

- Demand fluctuations are affected by consumption patterns and the organisation of production. For example, the fashion industry has been increasingly moving towards a greater number of collections per year. This results in shorter runs for manufacturers and greater uncertainty over the quantity of work; Just in Time (JIT) production increases fluctuations in production; closer relationships between subcontractors and subcontractees could result in reductions in demand fluctuations.
- Labour shortages are affected by overall economic demand, as well as by demographic changes. Supply is currently adequate, although this could change in an economic upturn.

Thus, whilst the case study evidence has shown how working-time practices may be used to address particular pressures, the development of these practices across the economy will depend, in part, on future economic developments.

Chapter 8

Summary and Conclusions

The aim of this research was to discover whether the growth in flexible working, which had taken place in the 1980s, had continued and whether there had been changes in employers' approach towards flexibility. The extent of promotion of flexible practices over the last decade or so in the management literature and by the government (including the subcontracting of public sector work) suggested that growth was likely to have continued. However, an important pressure for flexibility, labour shortage, had eased. Furthermore, the widespread dissemination of information on new managerial practices in general and flexible practices in particular may have encouraged change in managerial approaches towards labour use, a change which had been mooted (Atkinson and Meager, 1986) but had not occurred in the 1980s (Wood and Smith, 1987; McGregor and Sproull, 1991; Hunter and MacInnes, 1991; Casey, 1988 and 1991). With these pressures on employers, it was unclear whether flexible practices had continued to grow and whether management approaches were changing. It was therefore timely to investigate whether further change had occurred.

The study focused on numerical flexibility and flexibility of timing of hours of work. However, as different forms of flexibility may be complements or substitutes, other forms of flexibility (such as multi-skilling) were also considered. Using the Workplace Industrial Relations Surveys (WIRS) and the Labour Force Surveys (LFS), we were able to look at change in the use of certain flexible working-time practices over the last decade. Analysis of these surveys was supplemented with case studies, which explored further the nature of the changes and their rationale.

Although WIRS and the LFS were considered to be the most fruitful sources of national information, neither of these surveys was designed to explore flexible working patterns and it was recognised at the outset that they could supply only limited findings. A supplementary aim of the study was to identify gaps in current knowledge and areas where further research was needed. Despite the information which the LFS and WIRS provided, the limited scope of their questioning on working time and related practices highlights the dearth of nationally representative data on this topic. This seriously restricts our knowledge about the development of flexible practices. Appendix 4 discusses the types of data required for a better understanding of flexibility.

Changes in flexible working time

The study found that there had been a substantial increase in the use of flexible working time over the last decade. Growth was widespread, occurring in all working-time practices which could be examined using the Labour Force Survey and the Workplace Industrial Relations Surveys, with the exception of agency working. The number of people whose hours varied from week to week had increased particularly rapidly. Employees working variable hours had been the most common flexible working-time practice at the start of the decade and its growth resulted in this being the pre-eminent practice by a long way by 1994. Unfortunately, the information in the LFS does not explain the nature of fluctuation, although for many employees it may arise from variation in overtime hours. There were also large increases in the number of people working part-time and on a temporary basis. 'New' subcontracting had increased threefold, but from a small base. The use of subcontracting and the use of freelancers had spread across employers, but slowly, and most workplaces still neither used freelancers nor employees on short-term contracts.

Contrary to the widespread attribution of increased flexibility in the labour market to the growth of small firms, the study found that flexible working-time practices had grown most in larger establishments. Most dramatically, the doubling of the use of temporary workers in larger establishments (those with more than 25 employees) led larger establishments overtaking smaller in the use of this practice. Variable-hours working had been more common in larger establishments throughout the decade and showed slightly faster growth than in smaller establishments. Part-time working also grew faster in larger establishments, although it remains more common in smaller establishments.

An important question is whether the growth in flexible working-time practices signalled a change in approach by employers or whether it was merely a reflection of a shift in employment to industries and occupations where these practices had always been used. The clear message from the study was that most growth had been due to changes in employers' practices rather than due to a change in the industrial or occupational composition of the economy. The growth in temporary work and the use of variable hours was almost wholly attributable to a change in employers' practices, although a growth in industries which traditionally employed part-timers was responsible for some of the growth in part-time employment. However, for subcontracting and the use of freelancers, the data suggest that the main growth has been through employers who had already used these practices increasing their use, rather than the practice spreading extensively. The use of short-term contracts has increased slightly, mainly in the public sector where its use is concentrated. Outside the public sector its increase appeared to be concentrated among organisations with indications of a 'hire and fire' approach to management.

The degree of flexibility that exists in the labour market should not be exaggerated. Whilst the number of hours of work varies across individuals, the extent of variation in hours within and across organisations is not great. There is substantial clustering within small ranges of hours. Thus, whilst many aspects of working-time practices and numerical flexibility were found to be conditioned by product market and labour market pressures, these seemed to have little effect on the number of hours worked. This appears to be a major inflexibility in the labour market and may affect a number of major aspects of employment, for example, the number of jobs (and hence unemployment), the types (and number) of jobs available to women and to men, and the scope for more 'family friendly' working-time practices.

Convention, undoubtedly, plays a role in this clustering, but other employer or employee factors may also result in this seeming inflexibility. The case studies did identify some reluctance among employers to make use of particularly long hours of work and also a preference for full-time workers. However, these, and employee influences, need to be looked at in more detail if we are to understand the inflexibility over hours. For example, employees might seek to achieve a target number of hours as well as a target level of earnings and this could lead to a lack of variation in hours despite major variations in wage rates; and institutional influences, such as collective agreements on the working week, may lead to similarities in hours.

Factors affecting the type of working-time practices used

The increased emphasis on flexibility from various quarters, including management theorists and the government, set the context for the growth in flexible working-time practices. However, the types of practices in use by each employer were conditioned by historical practice and the circumstances peculiar to each organisation. Using new case-study research, together with analysis of WIRS and the LFS, the study found that the combination of flexible practices used by each employer resulted from a complex interaction between an organisation's external markets (product and labour), the nature of the product, the overall managerial approach and the complementarity and substitutability of practices.

Along with historical precedent, one of the stronger influences on working time was the pattern of product demand. The extent and timing of demand fluctuations and their predictability were very important in determining the type of working-time practice used. Where product demand fluctuated, the effect on the demand for labour (and hence on working-time practices) depended on the use of techniques to smooth production (for example, the use of stocks or the movement of services over time). A whole range of business approaches affect these patterns. For example, 'just in time' production increases labour demand fluctuations by its very nature of reducing the buffer between demand and production that stocks provide; marketing approaches, through changing the consumption cycle, may affect the pattern of labour demand (the clothing case studies provided examples of this: major buyers had changed from two collections per year to four or even six, reducing the contract size, increasing uncertainty and introducing more demand fluctuation); concentrating business into core products and divesting peripheral activities may reduce the ability to transfer employees across product areas and so increase fluctuations in the demand for labour. It is important to identify the extent of spread of these and similar practices as they have an important influence on the flexible working practices used.

Labour supply considerations came into play in two ways. Firstly, gender stereotyping meant that certain practices would not be considered for a predominantly male or predominantly female work group. Thus, in manufacturing, there was the belief that women did not wish to work overtime or at night, and that women and men had different preferences about when overtime was worked; across all sectors, temporary jobs and part-time working were seen as suitable for women and not men; and, as a response to labour shortage, increased pay and not changes in working-time seemed to be considered for men, but changes in working-time were a major response for female jobs. Apart from this stereotyping, labour supply only started to dictate the nature of practices in conditions of shortage.

This gender stereotyping of practices was based on employers' beliefs about men's and women's preferences. Whilst the stereotyping reflects the pattern of men's and women's work, it is unclear the extent to which it reflects preferences, rather than the opportunities offered by employers. It is particularly of note that differences were apparent across industries, suggesting, perhaps, that preferences over working time were not, in fact, gender specific. In a labour market which is occupationally segregated by gender, such stereotyping of working-time practices imposes severe constraints on the opportunities open to women and to men who hold different preferences. It also reinforces occupational segregation. Through the differential availability of part-time and temporary jobs it is likely to affect unemployment and dependence on benefits. In economic terms, it will be inefficient. It would be useful to understand more about these beliefs, including their basis and the validity of the assumptions.

Production methods, including the capital/labour ratio and work organisation, were important influences on the flexible practices used. Intensive use of freelancers and employees on short-term contracts were confined to industrial sectors where labour costs dominated other costs.

Whilst it was apparent that employers' practices were shaped by market and product considerations, the extent that practices matched these pressures depended on managerial sophistication and on the magnitude of the pressures (profitability and labour shortage) under which the organisation operated. It was apparent that some employers lacked information about the newer practices, restricting their ability to judge their benefits or the complexities of implementation. However, employers had substantial choice over the working-time practices used, as different combinations of working-time practices could be used to achieve similar outcomes. A number of practices were complements and substitutes for each other. Different practices relating to flexibility over the timing of work, over the number of hours worked, over the permanence of contracts and over the task mix of jobs could be grouped in different ways to match a range of circumstances. Similar organisations were found to employ different approaches to flexibility. This is an important finding, showing that there are a range of responses to the same circumstances and that modes of organising working-time and other practices are not determined uniquely by productivity pressures: there is scope for choice. Thus, employers' preferences were able to affect the practices in use and it was apparent that employers had a preference for full-time, permanent employment. Moreover, the implementation of different practices did not seem to be restricted by union power. Indeed, part of the recent increase in flexible practices, especially in the use of freelancers, may reflect a decline in unions' ability to resist temporary forms of work.

Future developments in flexible practices

There is a general belief that full-time, permanent jobs with set hours will decline and that more flexible forms will grow. Whilst this study does not contradict this scenario, it has presented evidence which should lead to circumspection in judgements about the extent and nature of growth in flexible working time.

The study identified factors which were likely to affect the growth of flexible practices in the future. These are listed below.

- The economic cycle: upturns are likely to lead to a slackening of cost pressures on employers, reducing the pressure to introduce flexible practices. However, they may also lead to greater labour supply pressures encouraging the growth of 'family-friendly' flexible practices.
- A continued increase in global competition would maintain pressure to minimise costs in some sectors and hence to develop flexible practices.
- Changes in product demand fluctuations, which might be caused by changes in consumption patterns and the organisation of production and which could result in greater labour demand fluctuations and uncertainty (as is happening in the fashion industry and with the spread of just-in-time production), or greater certainty (as is happening where closer relationships are being developed between contractors and subcontractors).
- Changes in policy in the public sector. There has been strong pressure to minimise costs: changes in such policy could affect the extent to which cost-minimising working-time practices are used.
- Changes in management preferences, which might be influenced by fashion and by the rate of dissemination of 'new' practices.

Thus, it is the argument of this study that economic factors are of primary importance in the changing pattern of use of flexible working-time practices. The advantages and disadvantages identified make it clear that certain practices may be more appropriate for a larger number of employers in particular economic circumstances than in other circumstances. Recent developments in working-time practices may owe much to a combination of recession (and excess labour supply), increased international competitive pressures, and policies towards the public sector. Predictions about future developments in working-time practices should be based on predictions about economic developments, rather than on the assumption that working time is an independently changing phenomenon.

However, the fact that employers have choice over practices means that the pattern of working-time practices may change not only in response to changing needs and pressures but also to changing preferences. These themselves may be subject to fashion. Fashions in human resourcing seem to be taken up with enthusiasm by 'leading-edge' employers, followed, over time, by other employers; subsequently, problems with new practices become evident and the practice falls out of favour or settles down to be used in more limited circumstances. Taylorist approaches to work, performance pay and flexitime are all examples of this pattern. It would be rash to assume that practices which have been subject to extensive promotion and have clear disadvantages as well as advantages, may not also be susceptible to this pattern.

Appendix 1

Classification of Activity by Industry

Details of classification of activity by industry used in Chapter 2

Abbreviated title used in tables	*Full description given in the Standard Industrial Classification (SIC) 1992*
Agriculture	Agriculture, Hunting, Forestry and Fishing
Oil and gas extraction	Extraction of mineral oil and natural gas
Other mining	Other mining and quarrying
Food, drink and tobacco	Food and beverages; Tobacco products
Textiles	Textiles
Leather	Leather products
Wood products	Wood and wood products
Paper, printing and publishing	Pulp, paper products, printing and publishing

continued

Details of classification of activity by industry used in Chapter 2 (continued)

Abbreviated title used in tables	Full description given in the Standard Industrial Classification (SIC) 1992
Oil refining and fuels	Solid and nuclear fuels, oil refining
Chemicals	Chemicals and man-made fibres
Rubber and plastic	Rubber and plastic products
Other mineral products	Other non-metallic mineral products
Metal products and metals	Basic metals and metal products
Machinery and equipment	Machinery and equipment
Electrical equipment	Electrical and optical equipment
Transport equipment	Transport equipment
Other manufacturing	Other manufacturing
Electricity, gas and water	Electricity, gas and water supply
Construction	Construction
Distribution	Wholesale and retail trade; repairs
Hotels and restaurants	Hotels and restaurants
Transport and communication	Transport and storage; Post and telecommunication
Financial services	Financial intermediation
Business services	Real estate, renting and business activities
Public administration	Public administration, national defence, social security
Education	Education
Health and social work	Health and social work
Other services	Other services

Appendix 2

Supplementary Tables
for Chapter 2

Tables are associated with the same numbered table in Chapter 2.

Table A2.1   Sample numbers, industry groups, Spring 1994 LFS

	Employees only*	Employees & home workers**	Employees & self-employed***
Agriculture	572	572	1211
Oil & gas extraction	106	107	113
Other mining	172	172	179
Food, drink & tobacco	1,203	1,203	1,241
Textiles	915	930	997
Leather	130	130	137
Wood products	178	178	219
Paper, printing & publishing	1,288	1,294	1,403
Oil refining & fuels	141	141	143
Chemicals	814	814	831
Rubber & plastic	611	614	648
Other mineral products	399	399	429
Metal products & metals	1,306	1,306	1,405
Machinery & equipment	1,231	1,231	1,275
Electrical equipment	1,519	1,526	1,583
Transport equipment	1,301	1,302	1,333
Other manufacturing	538	542	618

continued

Table A2.1   continued

	Employees only*	Employees & home workers**	Employees & self-employed***
Electricity, gas & water	586	586	593
Construction	2,552	2,555	4,525
Distribution	8,642	8,657	10,069
Hotels & restaurants	2,308	2,313	2,733
Transport & communication	3,518	3,520	3,950
Financial services	2,795	2,797	2,915
Business services	4,547	4,565	5,731
Public administration	3,954	3,956	3,982
Education	4,671	4,673	4,869
Health & social work	6,394	6,402	6,881
Other services	2,921	2,933	3,609
Total	55,312	55,418	63,622

*   cols 1–5 in Table 2.1
**   col 7 in Table 2.1
*** col 6 in Table 2.1

Source: Spring 1994 LFS

Table A2.3   Sample size, SEG, employees only, Spring 1994 LFS

	percentages
Employers & managers (large establishments)	6,510
Employers & managers (small establishments)	3,523
Professional workers	2,816
Intermediate non-manual	9.161
Junior non-manual	11,744
Personal service workers	3,247
Foreman/supervisor (manual)	2,743
Skilled manual	5,952
Semi-skilled manual	5,737
Unskilled manual	3,104
Farm managers	56
Agricultural workers	435
Military personnel	292
Occupations inadequately described	106
Total	55,426

Table A2.4   Sample numbers, employees only, industry groups, Summer 1993 – Spring 1994 LFS

	Summer 1993	Autumn 1993	Winter 1993	Spring 1994
Agriculture	605	614	569	572
Oil & gas extraction	161	144	105	106
Other mining	191	194	162	172
Food, drink & tobacco	1,326	1,323	1,196	1,203
Textiles	1,064	1,045	969	915
Leather	32	35	142	130
Wood products	617	595	177	178
Paper, printing & publishing	1,259	1,244	1,275	1,288
Oil refining & fuels	164	159	147	141
Chemicals	835	847	817	814
Rubber & plastic	590	586	596	611
Other mineral products	502	458	423	399
Metal products & metals	1,024	1,001	1,336	1,306
Machinery & equipment	1,859	1,734	1,279	1,231
Electrical equipment	2,016	1,918	1,529	1,519
Transport equipment	1,430	1,400	1,346	1,301
Other manufacturing	170	185	534	538
Electricity, gas & water	729	713	591	586
Construction	2,505	2,502	2,572	2,552
Distribution	8,557	8,606	8,779	8,642
Hotels & restaurants	2,440	2,434	2,261	2,308
Transport & communication	3,666	3,670	3,519	3,518
Financial services	2,415	2,349	2,803	2,795
Business services	4,236	4,206	4,526	4,547
Public administration	4,095	4,035	4,144	3,954
Education	4,338	4,574	4,531	4,671
Health & social work	4,042	4,039	6,411	6,394
Other services	5,873	5,814	2,906	2,921
Total	56,741	56,424	55,645	55,312

Table A2.5 Sample numbers, employees only, industry groups, Spring 1984 and Spring 1994 LFS

	Spring 1984	Spring 1994
Agriculture	679	572
Oil & gas extraction	107	106
Other mining	603	172
Food, drink & tobacco	1,449	1,203
Textiles	1,278	915
Leather	58	130
Wood products	546	178
Paper, printing & publishing	1,090	1,288
Oil refining & fuels	138	141
Chemicals	828	814
Rubber & plastic	484	611
Other mineral products	479	399
Metal products & metals	1,269	1,306
Machinery & equipment	1,517	1,231
Electrical equipment	1,917	1,519
Transport equipment	1,653	1,301
Other manufacturing	195	538
Electricity, gas & water	776	586
Construction	2,628	2,552
Distribution	6,443	8,642
Hotels & restaurants	1,982	2,308
Transport & communication	2,976	3,518
Financial services	1,760	2,795
Business services	2,477	4,547
Public administration	3,016	3,954
Education	3,385	4,671
Health & social work	2,807	6,394
Other services	3,632	2,921
Total	46,172	55,212

Table A2.7 Sample numbers, employees only, by size of establishment,
Spring 1984 and Spring 1994 LFS

	Spring 1984	Spring 1994
Under 25 employees	15,407	18,570
20 or more employees	30,765	36,265
Total	46,172	54,835

Table B2.4(i) Part-time shares, quarterly, employees only, by industry, Summer 1993 – Spring 1994 LFS

Industry	Summer 1993	Autumn 1993	Winter 1993	Spring 1994	Average	(Highest-lowest)/ lowest
Agriculture	23.6	23.4	21.0	20.7	22.2	14.1
Oil & gas extraction	1.9	1.4	3.3	3.1	2.4	136.4
Other mining	1.0	2.4	3.5	3.3	2.6	269.9
Food, drink & tobacco	15.5	14.4	12.4	12.7	13.8	25.4
Textiles	14.6	13.0	11.6	11.1	12.6	31.5
Leather	11.6	16.7	14.0	16.1	14.6	38.7
Wood products	6.5	5.7	5.1	7.8	6.3	52.0
Paper, printing & publishing	13.6	13.5	12.9	12.3	13.1	10.3
Oil refining & fuels	1.8	3.3	3.8	3.8	3.2	109.8
Chemicals	5.6	6.5	5.7	5.0	5.7	31.2
Rubber & plastic	8.6	8.1	8.6	8.5	8.5	6.0
Other mineral products	5.6	5.4	5.7	4.5	5.3	26.4
Metal products & metals	5.7	6.8	5.6	5.5	5.9	21.9
Machinery & equipment	6.6	6.3	5.8	5.6	6.1	19.1
Electrical equipment	5.7	5.2	5.6	6.7	5.8	27.6
Transport equipment	3.7	3.4	3.1	2.6	3.2	40.8
Other manufacturing	15.3	12.2	8.5	7.4	10.8	107.8
Electricity, gas & water	6.4	8.0	6.3	5.9	6.7	26.0
Construction	8.1	7.9	7.3	8.0	7.8	8.5
Distribution	39.4	39.6	39.8	39.9	39.7	1.3

continued

Table B2.4(i) continued

	Summer 1993	Autumn 1993	Winter 1993	Spring 1994	Average	(Highest-lowest)/ lowest
Hotels & restaurants	54.5	55.9	54.0	54.1	54.6	3.5
Transport & communication	9.4	9.8	9.8	9.9	9.8	5.3
Financial services	13.4	13.3	14.1	14.5	13.8	9.2
Business services	16.7	17.1	21.6	22.5	19.5	35.2
Public administration	13.4	13.3	14.7	14.1	13.9	9.5
Education	36.1	37.4	36.7	36.9	36.8	3.5
Health & social work	42.6	43.1	46.0	46.3	44.5	8.5
Other services	44.1	43.8	37.4	39.3	41.2	18.0
Total	24.6	24.9	25.1	25.4	25.0	3.5

Table B2.4(ii) Temporary shares, quarterly, employees only, by industry, Summer 1993 – Spring 1994 LFS

Industry	Summer 1993	Autumn 1993	Winter 1993	Spring 1994	Average	(Highest-lowest)/ lowest
Agriculture	13.3	11.2	7.4	7.7	9.9	80.3
Oil & gas extraction	13.7	11.0	11.2	9.0	11.2	52.6
Other mining	12.1	14.1	10.2	8.2	11.2	72.7
Food, drink & tobacco	6.4	6.6	5.0	3.4	5.3	96.8
Textiles	2.8	2.9	3.5	2.3	2.6	52.2
Leather	0.0	5.9	3.1	1.6	2.6	high
Wood products	1.6	2.4	2.5	3.7	2.6	131.3
Paper, printing & publishing	4.6	4.4	4.8	4.7	4.6	9.0
Oil refining & fuels	9.3	6.8	5.0	6.5	6.9	85.0
Chemicals	3.9	3.5	4.8	6.1	4.6	72.1
Rubber & plastic	4.2	4.0	2.8	3.0	3.5	47.4
Other mineral products	3.2	2.8	2.9	2.5	2.9	28.3
Metal products & metals	2.7	3.1	3.7	2.3	2.9	62.6
Machinery & equipment	4.6	4.6	2.8	3.6	3.9	62.9
Electrical equipment	4.8	4.8	5.3	4.7	4.9	12.4
Transport equipment	3.8	3.2	3.7	3.7	3.6	17.3
Other manufacturing	3.8	5.8	3.2	2.7	3.9	113.8
Electricity, gas & water	4.8	4.2	4.9	5.6	4.9	33.8
Construction	8.0	7.8	6.8	6.2	7.2	29.6
Distribution	4.9	4.5	5.0	4.0	4.6	26.9

continued

Table B2.4(ii) continued

	Summer 1993	Autumn 1993	Winter 1993	Spring 1994	Average	(Highest-lowest)/ lowest
Hotels & restaurants	13.6	12.6	11.4	10.6	12.1	28.2
Transport & communication	5.0	5.2	5.0	4.6	4.9	13.0
Financial services	3.8	3.4	3.5	3.4	3.6	11.5
Business services	7.3	7.2	6.9	7.1	7.1	5.8
Public administration	5.3	5.1	6.0	5.8	5.5	16.6
Education	13.4	14.9	15.1	15.8	14.8	18.0
Health & social work	7.5	7.4	7.1	7.3	7.3	5.5
Other services	9.5	8.9	9.7	11.5	9.9	29.1
Total	6.8	6.8	6.6	6.5	6.7	4.9

Table B2.4(iii)   Variable hours shares, quarterly, employees only, by industry, Summer 1993 – Spring 1994 LFS

Industry	Summer 1993	Autumn 1993	Winter 1993	Spring 1994	Average	(Highest-lowest)/ lowest
Agriculture	75.2	72.1	66.9	68.8	70.7	12.4
Oil & gas extraction	61.2	60.0	63.5	70.3	63.7	17.2
Other mining	53.5	54.4	57.9	56.3	55.5	8.1
Food, drink & tobacco	60.3	59.0	58.4	57.9	58.9	4.1
Textiles	41.4	41.5	41.0	41.9	41.5	2.2
Leather	58.6	58.1	40.2	38.3	48.8	46.0
Wood products	53.3	54.6	56.6	51.3	53.9	10.3
Paper, printing & publishing	58.6	59.3	60.9	60.0	59.7	4.0
Oil refining & fuels	60.4	63.8	64.1	63.3	62.9	6.2
Chemicals	60.5	58.8	57.3	59.0	58.9	5.6
Rubber & plastic	55.0	54.5	54.2	59.0	55.7	8.9
Other mineral products	57.1	57.3	57.7	57.9	57.5	1.4
Metal products & metals	55.3	55.0	58.6	58.8	56.9	6.5
Machinery & equipment	60.0	60.1	58.9	60.5	59.9	2.7
Electrical equipment	59.2	57.9	58.5	58.9	58.6	2.2
Transport equipment	55.4	56.8	57.2	55.7	56.3	3.3
Other manufacturing	45.9	51.5	49.1	54.8	50.3	19.4
Electricity, gas & water	58.6	61.1	66.3	65.8	62.9	13.1
Construction	55.8	57.1	56.4	58.2	56.9	4.4
Distribution	47.9	48.1	48.5	48.7	48.3	1.6

continued

Table B2.4(iii) continued

	Summer 1993	Autumn 1993	Winter 1993	Spring 1994	Average	(Highest-lowest)/ lowest
Hotels & restaurants	54.7	53.4	56.3	57.4	55.5	7.3
Transport & communication	65.4	67.2	66.6	66.8	66.5	2.8
Financial services	55.8	57.1	54.5	56.7	56.0	4.7
Business services	58.9	57.9	56.6	57.8	57.8	4.1
Public administration	61.8	61.6	61.4	62.2	61.8	1.3
Education	54.5	53.8	53.5	56.0	54.4	4.5
Health & social work	50.3	50.3	51.1	51.9	50.9	3.2
Other services	53.2	53.2	53.9	56.1	54.1	5.4
Total	55.5	55.5	55.3	56.3	55.7	1.5

Appendix 3

The Case Studies

In the *clothing* industry four case studies were carried out in:

- a long-established manufacturer of children's clothing, operating in a traditional, city-centre area of the clothing industry and employing 100 employees in a combined factory, office and showroom. Most machinists were women and worked a four-and-a-half day week, with periodic overtime and holiday working, some temporary workers and much reliance on the subcontracting of whole orders to cope with peak demand.
- a small, recently-formed family business in the same area producing small batches of household textile products such as ironing board covers. It employed 20 people, mostly female machinists, a third of whom worked part-time with a variety of starting and finishing times. Outworking was the main method of coping with the highly seasonal demand.
- the main factory of a large, multi-site manufacturer of high quality men's clothing, also based in a city with a long history of clothing manufacture. It employed around 300 machinists, all women, in a highly fragmented system of production. Until recently all production workers had been full-time, but several non-traditional working-time practices had recently been introduced, some to cope with changing demand, some at the behest of employees. The main response to seasonality remained, however, stockholding of finished goods and work in progress, plus the subcontracting of complete orders.

- a single-site company in the South-East, with 68 employees. The workforce was nearly all female. About half the 40 machinists and packers worked part-time; all other employees were full-time. Employees worked a four and one-half day week. The firm suffered a chronic shortage of machinists. Demand was highly seasonal, leading to an annual pattern of high levels of overtime followed by short-time working. To cope with peaks in demand, work was subcontracted to ex-employees working at home and, on occasions, to other companies.

In the *oil refining* industry the four case studies covered:

- the headquarters of a major international oil and chemicals company with over 500 employees on the out-of-town headquarters site. Over 90 per cent of the predominantly male workforce worked on permanent, full-time contracts with regular 9 to 5 working hours. A large variety of non-standard working-time practices had been introduced for very small numbers of employees, some at the request of established women employees.
- the main British refinery (of another international oil company) on a large coastal site and employing around 500 staff, 70 per cent of them plant operators working rotating shifts. The highly stable demand requiring continuous and predictable labour inputs necessitated few deviations from standard, full-time, permanent working. A few temporary workers were hired as a substitute for normal probationary arrangements, while ad hoc tasks were subcontracted.
- the second largest establishment of a small specialist oil and chemical processing company, situated in an industrial area of high unemployment and having a profitable, near-monopoly position in its niche market. Employing some 40 workers, mainly men, all full-time, the fluctuating demands for its short-cycle processing were mainly coped with by varying overtime, plus an informal flexitime arrangement operated by technical staff.
- a subsidiary of a US company, employing about 70 people in the South West of England. About half the workforce were production workers, working day-shifts. Production workers were male, whereas most of the other employees were female.

Only one employee worked part-time. The labour market was slack and recruitment and retention were unproblematic. The firm had been moving towards a core/periphery approach and multi-skilling. Many functions had been subcontracted. The slight fluctuations in demand were coped with through overtime and, in slack periods, redeploying production workers on general maintenance tasks.

In the *metal goods manufacturing* sector there were three case studies covering:

- a small but expanding specialist metal-machining company in new premises on an industrial estate, supplying high-precision, customised parts for a variety of manufacturers, mostly in small batches. Demand was short-term and unpredictable, leading to widely fluctuating amounts of overtime and weekend working and changes in the extent of night-shift working.
- a long-established supplier of metal fabricated components to the vehicle manufacturing industry, recently the subject of a management buyout, operating on a single city-centre site in the Midlands. Orders were long-term but subject to small short-term quantity modifications. The mostly male workforce of about 150 included around 100 semi-skilled production machinists and assemblers. Some simple components were assembled by homeworkers; short-term contracts were used for probationary purposes and there was occasional overtime working.
- a company with six sites across Britain. About two-thirds of its workforce of 2,000 were hourly-paid, all of whom were male. Nearly all employees work full-time, with hourly-paid, working day shifts. Overtime, night shifts, weekend shifts and, occasionally, short-time working are used to cope with fluctuations in demand. The company has started to expand after a period of contraction and additional employees are first recruited on a temporary basis.

Four widely differing organisations were studied in the *business services* sector:

- a small and shrinking consultancy company specialising in information technology design and implementation for large, public sector customers. The 10 professional staff frequently worked large amounts of unpaid overtime, only occasionally getting time off in lieu. A substantial pool of freelance consultants was drawn upon when projects could not be serviced with in-house staff. A few part-time staff were on variable hours arrangements which depended on the flow of work.

- the main site of a contract rework and repackaging company providing services for retailers on a very short order cycle. Variable demand was dealt with by a changing mixture of full and part-time jobs, casual and temporary workers (often students), agency temps, overtime and weekend working, plus occasional extra shifts.

- a training company, based in outer London, providing guidance and training for government schemes. Despite the uncertainty caused by an annual tendering round for training, most work is conducted by 50 permanent employees. Freelancers are used for small or irregular batches of work. Most of its employees are full-time and over half are female.

- a consultancy and training organisation spread across three sites in Britain. Three-quarters of its 20 employees were professionals, the rest secretarial. All secretarial staff were female and most professional staff male. All employees worked full-time. Demand was fairly constant, but occasionally additional training was taken on and subcontracted. Agency temps were used to cover secretarial peaks and absence.

Four companies in the *hotel and catering* industry were studied:

- a long-established restaurant in London, employing 45 people. Recruitment was difficult. Most staff were in their 20s and 30s and most were male. Most staff worked full-time and part-timers were employed where it was convenient to the job. Nearly all employees worked rotating shifts, with different shift systems for each occupation. A high degree of flexibility, at short notice, was required to cover variations in demand, with additional shifts and overtime common. Casuals were also used.

- a London hotel, which was part of a small chain. It mainly catered to the conference trade, resulting in some seasonal fluctuation in business. Ninety per cent of its 250 employees worked full-time. About 60 per cent were female. Temporary workers were used to cover long-term absence and a pool of casual workers were used for banqueting. Although many of its working-time practices were standard for hotels, it had been conducting a major review of staffing and service needs and altering its working time (and job content) accordingly.

- a high quality hotel, mainly catering to business customers. Nearly all its 300 employees worked full-time and worked on rotating day shifts. The hotel had eradicated split shifts in most jobs. Most employees were under 30 and 60 per cent were male. Staff are flexible over the hours they work and overtime is obligatory. Increased flexibility had been introduced through multi-skilling.

- a country hotel providing combined conference and leisure business. About three-quarters of its 85 employees were female and nearly half worked part-time. Staff worked rotating shifts across the week and split shifts were being eliminated. Variations in workload were addressed using overtime, except for banqueting which was staffed by casual workers.

In the *health* sector, the five health trusts studied were:

- a trust providing care for elderly people. Most work was long-term, community care, but residential care and acute services were also provided. It employed 3,000 people. Many nurses, the largest group of employees, worked part-time, which was a function of both labour supply and job tasks. Perhaps due to a slack labour market and extensive reductions in employment size, the trust had made few changes in traditional working-time patterns.

- a trust based in a large town in the South East, providing acute care. About half its 3,000 employees were nurses and 80 per cent of all staff were female. Recruitment difficulties had led to the introduction of a range of family-friendly working-time practices. Fluctuations in demand and absence were covered by the use of overtime, 'bank' and agency staff. The trust was conducting a review of skills, jobs and demand, leading to multi-skilling, changes in job tasks and work patterns.

- a trust whose main responsibility was a teaching hospital. Demand was fairly predictable. Cost pressures and extreme recruitment difficulties had led to a continuing review of working practices. All types of family-friendly practices were in use. In nursing, rotational shifts had been introduced and, to reduce costs, 'bank' staff were used in place of overtime. In some occupations, the working day had been extended by the introduction of shifts and multi-skilling introduced.
- a trust with a substantial share of psychiatric services. The trust had recruitment and retention problems. About half its staff were nurses, 80 per cent of employees worked full-time (including most nurses) and about two-thirds of employees were female. Rotational shifts had been introduced for quality reasons. Excess demand is covered mainly using 'bank' staff due to their cost advantage over agency staff and overtime. Job-sharing was normally available to all staff and annualised hours had been introduced in one occupation.
- a trust in a small northern town, covering all forms of hospital and community services. Recruitment was unproblematic in many occupations. A high proportion of nurses worked part-time; rotational shifts and annualised hours had been introduced. Fluctuations in demand were addressed using annualised hours, 'bank' nurses and additional hours from part-time staff; overtime was rare.

Appendix 4

The Need for Improved Data

One aim of the study was to identify gaps in current knowledge and areas where further research was needed. Despite the information which the LFS and WIRS provided, the limited scope of their questioning on working-time and related practices highlights the dearth of nationally representative data on this topic. This seriously restricts available knowledge about the development of flexible practices. Below, the types of data required for a better understanding are discussed.

Without nationally representative information on flexible practices and the factors conditioning their use, predictions about future developments and the implications of change are hazardous. Information on actual practices in use is particularly important, given the scope for employers' discretion and the consequent variation amongst similar organisations found in the study. Current limitations arise from the available national datasets because:

(i) The 1990 WIRS holds information on a small number of flexible practices only and is becoming increasingly out of date.

(ii) The LFS, as a survey of individuals and not of employing organisations, does not collect the detailed organisational information required.

(iii) In studying developments in employers' use of flexibility the categorisation of working practices commonly used in surveys of individuals is often inadequate or irrelevant. For example, temporary contracts were used by employers in a number of different circumstances (to cope with work fluctuations, to cope with growth, to cope with out of the ordinary work), with different rationales and different degrees of permanence. However, people employed on such contracts would often be unaware of the organisational circumstances giving rise to their temporary contract.

Similar information to that collected in the case studies needs to be collected on a national basis, covering all industries. A nationally representative survey of employing organisations, including information on working-time practices, use of numerical flexibility practices and the production, labour market and managerial context, would enable us to understand further the development of such practices and to anticipate future changes. Given the role that flexible practices play in the nature of work and the labour market, such information would make a major contribution to anticipating labour market developments and informing policy developments in relation to:

- the nature of jobs and employment;
- unemployment (for example, changes in the pattern of unemployment due to higher turnover of jobs and due to the take-up of temporary and part-time employment being impeded by the benefits system);
- the gender stereotyping of jobs and of different work practices and the balance and nature of female and male employment;
- family friendly working time (and its occupational availability) and the utilisation of the female workforce;
- job security and the precariousness of employment;
- occupational change and the nature of occupations;
- changing skill needs, for example, increased skills for self-employment or for job-changing;
- changing training and retraining needs, given the concentration of employer-provided training on employees in full-time, permanent jobs;
- productivity (for example, through the closer matching of labour supply and demand).

It would also be useful in anticipating changes which might need to be addressed by policy relating to social security and national insurance benefits. In particular, the benefits system for unemployed people discourages the take-up of part-time and insecure employment. The more it is the case that low-skilled jobs, in particular, develop patterns of employment discouraging access by unemployed people, the more the benefits system should address this issue.

An employer survey covering these issues would be highly complex. It would be important to capture the variations within employing organisations as well as between them and to capture interactions between practices and pressures. Such a survey would require extensive development work to ensure that each practice was investigated as part of a package and not in isolation. Development work should also cover the following:

(i)   development of a classification of flexible practices (neither ELUS nor regular national surveys provide the type of classification required). The case study findings provide a very good basis for developing such a classification.

(ii) questionnaire development on the pressures affecting the use of different practices. Again the case study work should be useful for this.

(iii) the development of approaches to handle both the *interaction* between practices and their *multiple* use at the individual level, at the job level and at the level of the employing unit.

(iv) investigation of how to approach questions relating to the nature of the job. This arises out of the complementary repackaging of tasks across jobs (for example, multi-skilling) with other aspects of flexibility. Approaches to classifying skills and jobs (other than SOC) should be investigated, along with other methods of examining changes in job content.

Finally, work would be required on the sampling approach, including methods to ensure the inclusion of the rarer practices.

Whilst the LFS as a survey of individuals is of limited use in collecting data on flexible working practices, it does offer scope on some aspects. In particular, further information on variability of working time would be useful. According to the LFS many employees' hours vary from week to week. However, an explanation of the fluctuation is only sought of employees who worked fewer hours than normal in the week to which their interview relates, that is, no explanation is sought from those working additional hours. Moreover, the only practice which is examined is short-time working. Other practices resulting in fewer hours are not identified. Given the size of the workforce affected by variations in hours and the degree of flexibility conferred on employers, it would be useful if questions in the LFS addressed this issue.

References

Atkinson J (1985) *Flexibility, Uncertainty and Manpower Management,* IMS Report No 89. Brighton: Institute for Manpower Studies

Atkinson J and Meager N (1986) *Flexibility in Firms: A Study of Changing Working Patterns and Practices.* Brighton: Institute for Manpower Studies

Beatson M (1995) *Labour Market Flexibility.* London: Employment Department Research Series No 48

Blanchflower D G and Corry B (1987) *Part-time Employment in Great Britain: An Analysis Using Establishment Data.* London: Department of Employment Research Paper No 57

Brannen J et al (1994) *Employment and Family Life: A Review of Research in the UK.* London: Employment Department Research Series No 41

Casey B (1988) *Temporary Employment: Policy and Practice in Britain.* London: Policy Studies Institute and the Anglo-German Foundation

Casey B (1991) 'Survey evidence on trends in "non-standard" employment'. In A Pollert (ed) *Farewell to 'Flexibility'? Questions of Restructuring Work and Employment,* pp179–199. Oxford: Basil Blackwell

Casey B and Creigh S (1988) 'Self-employment in Great Britain – its definition in the Labour Force Survey, in tax and social security law and in labour law', *Work, Employment and Society,* pp381–391. London: BSA Publications Limited

Casey B, Metcalf H and Lakey J (1993) 'Human Resource Strategies and the Third Age: Policies and Practices in the UK', *Age and Employment.* London: Institute of Personnel Management

Fernie S and Metcalf D (1995) 'Participation, Contingent Pay, Representation and Workplace Performance: Evidence from Britain', *British Journal of Industrial Relations,* 33 (3), pp379–415. Oxford: Blackwell Publishers

Hakim C (1985) *Employers' Use of Outwork*. London: Department of Employment Research Paper No 44

Hakim C (1987) 'Trends in the Flexible Workforce', *Employment Gazette,* pp549–560, November. London: HMSO

Hunter L, McGregor A, McInnes J and Sproull A (1993) 'The "Flexible Firm": Strategy and Segmentation', *British Journal of Industrial Relations,* 31 (3), pp383–407. Oxford: Blackwell

Hunter L and MacInnes J (1991) *Employers' Labour Use Strategies – Case Studies*. London: Department of Employment Research Paper No 87

McGregor A and Sproull A (1991) *Employer Labour Use Strategies: Analysis of a National Survey*. London: Department of Employment Research Paper No 83

Metcalf H (1990), *Retaining Women Employees: Measures to counteract Labour Shortages*. Brighton: IMS Report No 190

Millward N (1994a) *The New Industrial Relations?* London: Policy Studies Institute

Millward N (1994b) *The 1984–1990 Panel in the Workplace Industrial Relations Survey Series: Some Substantive Analysis and a Methodological Assessment*. London: Policy Studies Institute

Millward N, Stevens M, Smart D and Hawes W (1992) *Workplace Industrial Relations in Transition: the ED/ESRC/PSI/ACAS Surveys*. Aldershot: Dartmouth Publishing

Moreton M (1995) 'A Model of Labour Productivity and Union Density in British Private Sector Unionised Establishments'. London: University of Greenwich, mimeo

Naylor K (1994) 'Part-time working in Great Britain – an historical analysis', *Employment Gazette,* pp473–484. London: HMSO

Pollert A (1988) 'The Flexible Firm: Fiction or Fact?', *Work, Employment and Society,* September, pp281–316. London: BSA Publications Ltd

Walker C (1993) 'Transition to the New Standard Industrial Classification', *Economic Trends,* 472, pp88–92. London: HMSO

Watson G (1992) 'Hours of work in Great Britain and Europe: Evidence from the UK and European Labour Force Surveys', *Employment Gazette,* November, pp539–57. London: HMSO

Watson G (1994) 'The flexible workforce and patterns of working hours in the UK', *Employment Gazette,* pp239–247, London: HMSO

Wood D and Smith P (1987) *Employers' Labour Use Strategies – First Report of the 1987 Survey*. London: Employment Department Research Paper No 63